PHENOMENAL LOVE

The Greatest Force of All

HOWARD PARTRIDGE
BRENDA J. SELL

ISBN: 9798404946680

Dedication

To My Princess Denise for loving me unconditionally for four decades. You have always stood beside me, sometimes in front of me, leading me, and sometimes behind me, cleaning up my mess.

You have always been there for me.

I love you with all my heart.

Your Knight, Howard

Part 1
Phenomenal LOVE
Howard Partridge

Introduction
Phenomenal LOVE

The late American legend, Zig Ziglar told just about everyone he met to write a book. If you were a married man he would add, "and talk about your wife." He would then go on and on about his wife Jean who he referred to as "The Redhead".

I took Zig's advice and wrote my first book *7 Secrets of a Phenomenal L.I.F.E.* and I talked a little bit about my phenomenal wife Denise. Laurie Magers, who was Zig's executive assistant for over 38 years, did the first edit of that book. I was very grateful to have someone who knew Mr. Ziglar's work as well as Laurie to edit my first book.

As Laurie and I went back and forth during the editing process, I assumed she would tell me if something was especially good, or if there was anything that should not be in the book.

But she didn't.

Throughout the entire editing process, being the true professional she is, she only commented on grammatical issues, which were many since I grew up in "Lower Alabama"!

While she never encouraged or discouraged any part of the book, I was worried it wasn't good and she just didn't want to tell me.

After she finished the project, I hesitantly asked her what she thought about the book. "Oh, Howard the book is great! But what your wife said was a scream!"

There you have it.

Zig obviously knew what he was talking about when he said to talk about your wife!

Shortly after the book came out, I was on stage at one of my conferences, talking about the book. Denise was in the audience that day and began talking back while I was on the stage. She is known to do that from time to time. "Honey my girlfriends and I were looking at your new book today and found a typo on the cover."

"On the *cover*?" I exclaimed in disbelief.

"Yeah, it should be called *The Secrets of a Phenomenal W.I.F.E.!*" She quipped.

The audience *loved* that. Once again Denise stole the show! But as I began thinking about it, I started writing this book. The original title was to be *The 4 Secrets of a Phenomenal W.I.F.E.*

A phenomenal **W.I.F.E.** is...

Wise – they make good decisions.
Influential – they have a positive impact on others.
Faithful – they remain persistent and consistent through the trials of life.
Excellent – as Proverbs 31 points out, they *excel* in life's responsibilities.

But as I got to thinking about these four words, I realized how much they apply to *all* of us.

Therefore, this book is for everyone.

All of life is about relationships, and the only sure thing that can make a relationship work is *love.*

Would you agree that all humans want to love and to be loved?

If that's true, why do we have so many relationship problems?

INTRODUCTION

Love is the one thing that everyone wants more of, but it's the one thing that seems so scarce in our society today.

Why is that?

Why is it that love seems to be so misunderstood?

Why are people so selfish in our modern world?

Love is the one thing that makes the heart sing and it can heal like nothing else. At the same time, it's something that seems to hurt like nothing else.

The world would probably define love as a feeling, but this book is about something deeper than the world's definition of love.

Phenomenal Love is a love that can only come from God. Phenomenal Love is not some light feeling or emotion. We're talking about a phenomenal *commitment*, that in turn produces an amazing fruit called joy, and an unbelievable sense of fulfillment.

The hurt and pain that we experience when we don't receive the love we expect has more to do with expectations and hidden fears. Therefore, while emotions are certainly involved, we have to exercise a little emotional intelligence to discover where those feelings are coming from.

Hurts and disappointments are coming from a place of fear, while joy, fulfillment and hope come from a place of faith.

So, how do we experience phenomenal love?

How do you share it?

In this book, we'll talk about that. And we'll talk about how Phenomenal Love can make a difference in your life and the lives of those around you.

Before we go any further, you may be wondering why would I attempt writing to you about such a big, meaningful, deep subject such as this?

After all, I'm certainly not exactly the most qualified person to talk about love! I wrote the majority of this book six years ago, but I didn't release it because I didn't feel worthy to write it. I mean who *is* qualified to write a book on the most important subject in the entire world?

No one.

But maybe everyone.

One person I would consider to be more than qualified is Brenda Sell Jones or *Senior Grandmaster Brenda J. Sell Jones,* if you're addressing her as the highest-ranking American female in Tae Kwon Do in the world, which she is.

I've seen her put a grown man on the floor in about a second during a martial arts demonstration at one of our member retreats. And he was a fairly large man. As my buddy was laying on the floor, Rick Jones, one of our coaches was in the audience. "I wouldn't wanna be married that woman." He quipped under his breath. Well, as the old saying goes, "be careful what you say". He ended up getting married to Brenda. And I was the best man at the wedding.

But that's another love story for another time.

The force of martial arts is just one side of Brenda. I have also witnessed her gently share God's love with others. I've seen how she loves God. I've seen her love others, and pray for them diligently I am a grateful recipient of her powerful prayers.

I also had the privilege and honor of walking through a difficult time with Brenda as she battled breast cancer. And overcame it! I have watched in amazement as she teaches her Tae Kwon Do students about God and about His love.

That's why I asked Brenda to include her powerful study called *The Forces of Love,* as part of this book, which she graciously agreed. As you will see, she is much more qualified to talk about love. She is much more "loving" than I am. I'm a hard-charging business owner, and a high "D" on the DISC Model of Human Behavior, so my love for others doesn't shine as brightly as Brenda's does.

Surely, there are many books available on the subject of love, but I have felt compelled for some time now to share this with those I am called to serve. And I've been the recipient of an abundance of love and favor from God and many others, so I've experienced phenomenal love.

In addition to the love I have received from so many, I also been blessed to see many lives change as they respond to God's love and the love others have demonstrated to them.

My experience is that love truly does "conquer all".

As one human being to another, I just seek to share the pot of gold that has changed my life, in hopes that it will help you love and be loved more deeply than ever before.

I hope to simply share a few trials, truths, and triumphs that I've encountered over the years in hopes that they may help you on your love journey. I hope to challenge you to go deeper than worldly love and experience the unconditional, phenomenal love that we can only experience through God Himself.

The first thing I want to share is that God *is* Love and you were created in His image. You were created to love and to *be* loved by God. As my friend Dr. Caroline Leaf likes to say "you were wired for love".

The reason God created you was to love you! He created you for the same reason people have children. We have children to love them. We hope they will love us back. We are wired to *experience* love.

I often call myself "the most blessed man on the planet" because I have received so much love from so many. I have received so much favor from so many people in my life that I wake up every day with an incredible sense of gratitude, joy, and fulfillment.

I want everyone to experience that.

If you are one of those that have loved me, thank you from the bottom of my heart.

I love you. Phenomenally.

Chapter 1
The One Choice

Many years ago, Denise and I were having problems in our marriage. We weren't getting along and we had different visions about how life was to be lived. We were both frustrated. We were experiencing a lot of pain and not much happiness.

My oldest brother Larry and his wife Dorothy, who have a phenomenal marriage, were visiting us for a long weekend. They immediately picked up on the drama. Over breakfast, my brother asked me a piercing question.

"Do you love her?"

Before I share how I answered that question, let me set the stage for what led up to our marriage difficulties. When Denise and I first started dating, I was a pretty wild young man. I wasn't even twenty years old yet. But I wanted to settle down. I wanted a normal life with someone a little more down to earth. I could write a volume of books about the many, crazy girlfriends I had up until that point.

Denise was four years older than me. We met at a private club we both worked at. I was a lunchtime bartender (and I was a waiter at another restaurant at night). Denise was in membership sales. Can you already see the gap in maturity and life choices?

I invited Denise to my twenty-first birthday party. She didn't know how old I was. When she realized I was four years *younger* than her, she immediately began looking for the door to leave. I'm still not sure what the big deal about a four-year difference is, but I guess when you're twenty-something it is. At least for the older one. Now that we are in our sixties, it's not a big deal.

We got married three years later. I was twenty-three and she was twenty-seven. We had a few immediate problems. She didn't realize how much I was addicted to marijuana. She hated it. When we first got married, I was still a waiter, and when I got off work, instead of coming home immediately, I would go smoke pot with the boys and go to a pool hall or some place. I tried to be quiet when I slipped in the door afterward, but she was always awake. "Howard?" "Yes, Denise?" "Are you high?"

Silence.

After three more years, a miracle happened. The first of many as it turns out after I gave my life to God. The first miracle was that my marijuana habit was immediately gone! I had tried to quit many times before without success. But now, the desire was completely, utterly gone! Vanished! I never had an inkling for it ever again in my life. I can't even stand the smell of it today. It smells like dung to me.

Another miracle was about to come. By this time, Denise was done with me. When I got saved, she was at her parents' house in New Jersey for a "visit". I didn't know it at the time, but she was not planning on coming back! Although she didn't understand what the "Jesus" thing was all about, at least it was *something.* Something different. After confirming that I would be at home at night (in my right mind, not high), she returned home. God not only saved my soul, but He saved my marriage too! God's timing and His mercy is amazing!

But then, I got addicted to Jesus. Now I wasn't high and I wasn't out playing pool, but I was at the church building *all* the time. The "religious zealot" period lasted a few years, and then Denise and I had a good stretch of years.

Until...

I got involved with a ministry that had changed my life. It was a way of doing church that most people didn't understand. It was powerful, life changing and exciting. For me. But not for Denise.

I was convinced I was supposed to go into that ministry full time. I felt like I was supposed to travel with the leaders of this group and to devote the rest of my life to this work. Denise didn't buy into the ministry *at all.* In fact, she was convinced I was *not* supposed to do that. We didn't agree on very much at that time, and we argued a lot.

I asked the leader of that organization to counsel us. He was a brilliant man and I thought if anyone could help us, he could. He was very direct. There was no sugar-coating with him. I liked that. In fact, when it comes to coaching or counseling, my posture is to be completely open and trusting. Just put me on the operating table, "and cut out all the evil" is my attitude. And by the way, be sure to yank the root out!

When it comes to spiritual things, it doesn't matter how painful it is to me. I want all the bad stuff out, so I can have as much of the good stuff as possible. I tend to be incredibly open when it comes to mentoring. That was refreshing to the leaders of this group.

But Denise isn't like that. First, as with anyone you counsel, you need to build some rapport first. You need to build trust. He and I already had a great relationship, but he didn't really know Denise. And he didn't realize that she really didn't like him, or trust him to begin with.

Not only that, in her mind, *he* was the one that was keeping her husband from her. I was deeply committed to this man and his work. I went to every service, every event, every group, and every outreach that I could get to.

But my family was suffering.

After listening to each of us explain our difficulties, he finally turned to Denise and said "Woman, you've got problems." I was shocked that he was so frank and forward with her so quickly. I braced myself for the impact. I mean, you have to understand that you're talking to an *Italian* from *New Jersey!* Not exactly the most reserved, submissive type of person in the world.

This man was a seasoned pastor with decades of experience, a veteran missionary and the first person to teach me about personality types. How could he *possibly* make such a rookie mistake like that?

Denise went silent. When an Italian from New Jersey goes quiet, you *know* you have a problem! After asking him to leave, and quietly shutting the door behind him, she turned to me and let me know in no uncertain terms, "Choose him or me."

What?

You've got to be kidding! Choose the ministry that I think is the best thing that ever happened to the church – the organization I'm ready to give the rest of my life to – give it up? Just like that? I couldn't even speak to the man. Just having a conversation with him, was crossing the line that Denise had drawn in the sand.

I was hurt, dejected, and angry. Why couldn't Denise see what I saw? Why would she keep me from reaching more people for Christ and helping people get free spiritually?

Why didn't she get it?

Of course, I chose my marriage over that ministry, but I wasn't happy about the ultimatum. Here I was, angry with Denise, angry with my mentor for being too harsh with her, and angry at God for the first time in my life.

How could I be angry with *God*? Before that time in my life, I probably would have said that anyone who could be angry toward God probably wasn't a Christian at all. When I think about it now, I realize that I was the one who was wrong. Maybe Denise was too, but she saw things I didn't see. Looking back, I should have known I was wrong. Here I was neglecting my family for the ministry. Can I tell you something? That is not what God wants from you. He doesn't want you to be religious, He wants you to have a relationship with Him and to love your family.

Back to the breakfast table with my brother.

I finally replied to his question, "Do you love her?" with...

"Define love."

Isn't that the problem? We all have our own definition of love. Most people would define love as having feelings for someone. We hear the term "falling in love." While that is a real feeling, it's not the definition of love.

Often times, people describe love and happiness in the same sentence. Today, our culture is more concerned with our own "happiness" than what true love really means. If you've ever been in love, you also know that love can make you downright miserable! Especially if the one you love doesn't respond the way you think they should.

The Word of God has a lot to say about love. In fact, "the love chapter" is often recited at weddings...

Love is patient, love is kind, it is not jealous; love does not brag, it is not arrogant. It does not act disgracefully, it does not seek its own benefit; it is not provoked, does not keep an account of a wrong suffered, it does not rejoice in unrighteousness, but rejoices with the truth; it keeps every confidence, it believes all things, hopes all things, endures all things. Love never fails. (1 Corinthians 1:4-8a)

If you look closely at the words in this passage, there's very little about happiness, feelings, or emotions. Did you see anything that says if you aren't "happy" that you should remove a person from your life so *you* can be happy?

No.

This is one of the problems with the New Age movement in our culture. Get rid of the people in your life who don't bring you peace, is the idea of the day. I'm sorry to say, but that is a weak cop out.

How about this instead... choose to love people anyway. Be strong in love, so you can *help* the so-called "toxic" people. Help them experience love. True love. How about surrounding yourself with people who truly love you, that can strengthen you to the point where you no longer feel you are a victim. At least be in a place where you can stand your ground and not shut them out of your life.

Everyone agrees that true love is lacking in our society. You can't get through very many popular songs that don't include the longing for love. Everyone wants it, but few really understand it. There's an attack on traditional values today. There's an attack on committed relationships in our society. Our media-driven society dictates what love is, and what is right or wrong.

Love is not a mushy-gushy feeling. The romantic type love is only one type of love. I certainly don't mean to discount those feelings because they are very real, but at the end of the day, when the feelings wane, and you're faced with everyday life, like taking out the garbage, or being patient with someone who isn't nice to you, or dealing with an illness, emotion alone won't see you through. In fact, it may cause you more pain than joy.

But true love – *phenomenal* love is a commitment, that even though it may be painful at times, it produces something more important than "happiness". It produces a joy and a peace that surpasses understanding.

Phenomenal Love produces a deep level of fulfillment. When you serve others, you will be "happy". That's how God made us.

At sixty-one years of age, I have witnessed the devastating transformation of America that began with the rebellion of the 1960's. We went from love being seen as a commitment to a fleeting emotion.

We went from family values of honor and respect to "do your own thing" – "do what makes you happy". There is a specific, intentional attack on traditional values that were originally formed by God's Word.

I understand that there were problems back then. I understand that people were discriminated against. I understand that there was hate and oppression of a vulgar nature in our society at that time.

But in my humble opinion, the rebellion of the sixties overcorrected and brought a new set of values that much of our world buys into today. People move in together before they get married to make sure they will be "happy". If you get married, and you aren't happy, then you can just get divorced. If you're no longer in love, you just choose someone else that you "fall" in love with.

Is that really love?

Is that really what we're after?

Will trading your spouse in for a new model really fulfill you? Will trying to change your spouse going to make you happy? Is having an affair going to make you happy? Even if you get a new spouse and you feel "happier", you give up the bigger benefit that trumps happiness every time. What is that? Joy and fulfillment.

Is running away from someone going to help?

True joy and fulfillment are what you get when you choose to serve God by serving others. When you choose to serve, rather than just serving yourself, you'll not only experience, joy and fulfillment, but you'll be happy too!

You see, happiness is a by-product of choosing to love others, whether you think they deserve it or not. The goal is not to be happy. The goal is to serve. When you serve, you'll be happy. Happiness is the result.

Will kicking people out of your life because they don't "serve you", make you happy? No. It's more likely that you'll end up with a lot of regret because you have not understood the true meaning of love.

The greatest act of love in human history was when Jesus Christ gave His life for us. Do you think Jesus felt good when he died on the cross? Was he "happy and light" when the spikes were driven through his hands and his feet? I know that's harsh, but it's worth thinking about.

The unbelievable joy and fulfillment that came because of his death is amazing. Amazing Grace. You see, the "feeling" came *after* the sacrifice. When I decided to commit to my marriage, to be a better husband, and to commit to what *God says* instead of what *I felt,* more joy and fulfillment came to my life.

Again, I am not the perfect person to talk about love or marriage, but I *have* managed to keep a phenomenal woman as my wife for over thirty-seven years. And of course, that says more about her than it does me (If you know both of us, you know what I mean).

But what if I had not begun to understand what love truly is, we would have a terrible marriage, or worse, we wouldn't have a marriage at all.

We have a phenomenal marriage today because of ONE thing: We chose to be committed to God and His Word. We chose to commit to one another. We never considered divorce. We are two entirely different people, with many different interests and ways of looking at things, but we decided to trust what God says about the subject, rather than going with our own opinions.

Denise and I both are very independent and our marriage might even look a little different than the "model" marriage. Some marriages are obviously blissful from the outside. There are those that see their mate as their "everything" if you will. I really admire that.

Denise and I aren't like that.

Our marriage works because at the end of the day, we are *committed* to each other. And that's what love really is. It's a commitment. It's much more than that, but when you love someone, you're committed to him or her, regardless of how you feel about the circumstances.

Zig Ziglar said, "The chief cause of failure and unhappiness is trading what you want most for what you want now." What do we want most? Joy and fulfillment – to know that our lives matter. We live in a "now" generation that taps it's foot in front of the microwave.

What do *you* want most? Temporary happiness? Or long-lasting joy and fulfillment? Do you believe in God? Do you want a phenomenal relationship with God? To walk closely with Him? Is that what you want *most*? If the answer is yes, why would you jeopardize that relationship for what you want now?

Anytime we have relationship issues, we should look at ourselves first. Instead of living selfishly, let's allow God's love to live through us. If any of us want to have a more fulfilling relationship, we must fight against the schemes of the enemy.

We cannot just let the values of today's society attack and overcome us. Today, our society feeds on an extravagant buffet of sensuality. What society in its right mind would allow their children to take in X-Rated material on a daily basis? Yet, that's what we do.

Like sheep to the slaughter.

Yes, true love - phenomenal love - is under attack. We must choose to fight. And what weapons will we fight with? The Truth. God's Truth. As Jesus said "The truth shall set you free."

The most important outcome of true love is this...

When you endure the trials and tribulations of life, God molds you into the person He wants you to become. And that is the ultimate success in life. To become the person God created you to become.

As you choose to commit and sacrifice for others, treating them as more important than yourself, you will receive the benefits of trusting God. You will become a stronger person. You will become the best version of yourself.

This doesn't mean you become everyone's slave. I'm not talking about doing what other people expect you to do and being like they expect you to be. I'm talking about serving those you are called to serve.

Choose to love. It is the one choice that will never fail you.

Chapter 2
The Two Commandments

A rich young ruler came to Jesus and asked Him how to obtain eternal life. Here's the story from Scripture:

And someone came to Him and said, "Teacher, what good thing shall I do so that I may obtain eternal life?" And He said to him, "Why are you asking Me about what is good? There is only One who is good; but if you want to enter life, keep the commandments."

Then he said to Him, "Which ones?" And Jesus said, "You shall not commit murder; You shall not commit adultery; You shall not steal; You shall not give false testimony; Honor your father and mother; and You shall love your neighbor as yourself." The young man said to Him, "All these I have kept; what am I still lacking?" Jesus said to him, "If you want to be complete, go and sell your possessions and give to the poor, and you will have treasure in heaven; and come, follow Me." But when the young man heard this statement, he went away grieving; for he was one who owned much property.

And Jesus said to His disciples, "Truly I say to you, it will be hard for a rich person to enter the kingdom of heaven. And again, I say to you, it is easier for a camel to go through the eye of a needle, than for a rich person to enter the kingdom of God."

When the disciples heard *this*, they were very astonished and said, "Then who can be saved?" And looking at *them*, Jesus said to them, "With people this is impossible, but with God all things are possible."

Jesus knew this man's heart. He knew that he loved money and power more than God. In fact, the man actually lied to Jesus in that passage! Did you catch it? He said he had kept all of those commandments from his youth. Impossible! There are six hundred commandments in the bible, and certainly no man on earth has ever kept even the top ten!

Except Jesus. He was the perfect man. And God sent Him to relieve us from the Law. Scripture teaches us the law was *added* because of man's transgressions. The Law was introduced so that man would realize he *needed* God!

When asked about their faith, many people, Christians or not, might say something like, "I go by the Ten Commandments." But if you asked them to recite them, they probably couldn't.

And if the Ten Commandments are the standard, you have already failed.

All of us have.

So, instead of focusing on the *Ten* Commandments, why don't we focus on the *Two* commandments? There are several occasions recorded in Scripture where Jesus said there were "two commandments" that everything else hinges upon. And both of them have to do with love.

The first commandment is...

You shall love the Lord your God with all your heart, and with all your soul, and with all your mind.

In other places, He also said, "with your strength" or "with your body." Man is spirit, soul, and body. In this book, I want to unpack how these three parts interact as we strive to love God. But more importantly, how He loves you, which unlocks the Love of God in your life.

And the second commandment is...

You shall love your neighbor as yourself.

Although this is obvious, I think we would all agree that we all fall short.

Especially here in America. I know I do. So, if I fall short of it, how can I teach you about it? I can't. But God's Word can.

In order to get us on the same page, we have to determine what love is, Who God is, and who we are. Every human being has these values…

Here's my philosophy about love, gleaned from Scripture…

God is Love.

Therefore, any definition the world gives you, if God isn't included, it isn't Phenomenal Love.

There are three words used for love in Scripture. The New Testament was written in Greek, so let's take a look at the Greek words for love…

1. agape (unconditional love)
2. philia (friendship)
3. storge (natural affection)

Humans have the capacity to love.

Although the earth is phenomenal, and animals are an amazing creation of God, He made humans different. We are created in His image. Unlike animals, humans have a creative mind like God. Have you ever seen a dog build a skyscraper? Have you ever seen a gorilla build a spaceship? I don't think so. Humans also have the capacity to love. A domesticated dog may seem like "man's best friend" but I'm sorry to say that the affection a dog has, is purely selfish on their part. Sorry!

The reason we are so enamored with the "love" of a pet, is they don't seem to do the horrible things that man does. I've never seen a Nazi cat create a holocaust. Which brings me to the next part.

Humans have the capacity to hate.

We live in a fallen world. Remember Adam and Eve? Sin separated mankind from God. We were born into a sinful, fallen world and in our flesh, we have taken on that nature. We are born sinners!

But that doesn't change the fact that you were created to *be* phenomenal. It just means that you have to take a simple step to receive the love that God offered you through His Son Jesus. When you come to know Him, He changes your nature when His Holy Spirit begins to live inside of you.

God loves you.

John 3:16 says "For God so LOVED the World, that He gave His only begotten Son, that whoever BELIEVES in Him shall not perish, but HAVE everlasting life."

You are a new creature in Christ.

When we accept God's gift – the sacrifice of His Son and we invite Jesus into our hearts, we BECOME a new creature IN Christ. In my book *Think and Be Phenomenal*, I list 73 Scriptures that reveal the true identity of those in Christ.

God loves *through* you.

Once you accept Christ, He is IN you. And it means that when The Holy Spirit lives through you, God is loving THROUGH you.

You cannot do it alone.

True love, phenomenal love, cannot exist in the flesh. Sure, we feel affection through our emotions, but true, unconditional love, can only come through God. As a believer, God is in you. You have the power within you to love God and to love others.

Carrying out these two commandments is a daily, hour by hour journey for *all* of us. And it will be for the rest of our lives. I hope sharing the experiences I've been blessed to have in my life will help you experience a love that is nothing less than phenomenal.

The word phenomenal means very remarkable or extraordinary. God's love toward us is phenomenal. May we love others as phenomenally as He loves us.

Chapter 3
The Three Persons

After Jesus left the earth, he promised that He would send the Holy Spirit. Ten days later, the disciples were all together and God's Holy Spirit fell on 120 believers that were all together. Over 3,000 people got saved that day. In order for us to know God, we should understand the nature of God as well.

I am not a pastor, but simply a fellow believer on the journey with you. Scripture tells us that there are three persons in the Godhead: The Father, the Son and the Holy Spirit. In Genesis God said "Let's make man in Our image". That Hebrew word *Elohim*, means three or more.

Some people refer to it as the Trinity. Some groups point out that the word trinity isn't mentioned in the bible and therefore consider Jesus to be a creation of God, not part of God. I hope this isn't too much theology for you, but one God in three persons is the way to think about it. God is one. How can that be if God is one?

Here's an illustration: h2o is one compound but can express itself in three ways: liquid (water), vapor (steam), or solid (ice).

And if God is Love, then each of the three persons, expresses Love in different ways. The Father is on the throne and is to be worshipped. The Son (the Lamb of God) sits at His right hand and became a man to reconcile us to the Father. And the Holy Spirit is given to believers so that He can love *through* us. Before Jesus gave His life to reconcile us to the Father, the Holy Spirit could not inhabit mankind. I know that is a mystery. This is the mystery of Christ.

I know there is a lot of theology in those few short sentences, but if we are going to experience Phenomenal Love, then we should know the One who created us. We are also triune beings. We are spirit, soul and body. When we are born, we are still-born spiritually.

When God puts his Holy Spirit in us, we have the capacity to allow God to live through us. We have been made brand new in our spirit through *salvation.* However, we still live in our fleshly body, and have a soul (our mind, will and emotion) that needs to be *sanctified.*
That is what the Holy Spirit does. As we walk by the Spirit instead of in the flesh, God cleanses our soul over time. Spiritually, we are clean. Holy. Set apart. We have been transferred from the domain of darkness into the kingdom of light.

The battle is in the mind. And for the mind. We have been given the mind of Christ, but we must choose to use it. In order for God to love through us, we must make a choice to allow him to do it.

I believe the Word of God is truth. I personally and wholeheartedly believe that God inspired every word in the bible and there are no mistakes. Regardless of what people say about how the books of the bible were put together, I choose to believe that God guided those decisions.

After all, if there is no standard to follow, we can all make up our own minds and go with our own opinions. I choose to believe that there is *one* truth, not "your" truth and "my" truth.

Unfortunately, due to the cultural attack, many believers don't know Scripture. Christians themselves don't really know what the bible actually says. Unbelievers don't really know what Christians truly believe either.

There are so many religions and factions, and those outside the church don't really know what Scripture says either. They know "Christian religion" which is one of the biggest enemies of Christianity, just like the Pharisees were in Jesus' day.

Many believers and unbelievers react to any kind of godly instruction with "we just need to love each other". Well, that's true, but if we don't know what love is, how can we do that?

And if there is no truth, how can we love? Scripture tells us to tell to *truth in love*. If we don't know the truth then how can we love? The Apostle Paul said that the Word of God is for instruction in the truth. Jesus said "you shall know the truth, and the truth shall set you free."

Scripture instructs us that "it was for freedom that you were set free, but don't just use that freedom to serve yourself, but to serve others."This doesn't mean you can't have nice things. It just means we need to be rich toward God. It means you don't keep all the blessings God gives you for yourself to serve yourself. Help others.

If God is Love, we should understand His love letter to us. It's called the Holy Scriptures. We should know what we believe.

The best way I can concisely relate what Christians actually believe is ironically *not* in the bible per say, even though Scripture teaches each and every one of these points. It is called *The Apostle's Creed* and was created by the early church as a statement of faith. It is a statement of the basic tenants and doctrines of the Christian faith.

THE APOSTLE'S CREED

I believe in God,
the Father Almighty,
Creator of heaven and earth,
and in Jesus Christ, his only Son, our Lord,
who was conceived by the Holy Spirit,
born of the virgin Mary,
suffered under Pontius Pilate,
was crucified, died and was buried;
he descended into hell;
on the third day he rose again from the dead;
he ascended into heaven,
and is seated at the right hand of God the Father Almighty;

from there he will come to judge the living and the dead.
I believe in the Holy Spirit,
the holy universal Church,
the communion of saints,
the forgiveness of sins,
the resurrection of the body,
and life everlasting. Amen.

Everything I share in this book comes from this foundation of belief, so if you are a believer in Jesus Christ, you probably have a little more comfort that I'll be moving in a direction you can buy into. If you are not a believer yet, I'll let you choose how you want to proceed.

The Father, the Son and the Holy Spirit is the perfect example of phenomenal love. In Him you find Truth, Forgiveness and Power.

Most people define Christianity as a religion. It's not. It's a faith. What's the difference? Religion is a set of rules *about* God. Faith is a relationship *with* God. Religions teach you to "do" this or that to get favor from the "god" of that religion.

True Christianity is not a religion. There are many "Christian religions" but it is not a religion. Christianity is a faith that can be summed up in a famous passage called John 3:16.

For God so loved the world that He gave His only begotten Son, that whoever believes in Him should not perish, but have everlasting life.

There are two key words in this passage:

1. Loved. 'For God so *loved* the world...' The world is you and I. "that He gave". God gave first. "His only begotten Son". When you understand the true gospel, you understand that Jesus Christ, all God and all man existed with the Father from all eternity and was the only man that walked the earth that was born of the Holy Spirit, you will begin to understand this faith.

2. Believes. "That whosoever *believes* in Him…" Belief means that we trust Him. It means to cling to Him, to embrace Him, to glorify Him by expressing His values. We cling to God. Christianity is not a religion *about* God, it's a relationship *with* God.

Recently I read a book that defined belief as "beloved". In other words, to believe means to be loved. That's interesting because God gives us belief by loving us first. We believe by *faith* that *He* gave. When we know Him, we are his beloved.

The word believe in John 3:16, means to be committed to. Love is a commitment. Therefore, God loved us, and by believing, we commit to Him. We commit to that truth. We love Him because He first loved us.

Chapter 4

The Four Secrets of a Phenomenal W.I.F.E.

Again, this book isn't just about marriage. This chapter applies to all of us!

A Phenomenal W.I.F.E. is...

Wise
Influential
Faithful
Excellent

WISDOM

"We have more knowledge than ever before, but we lack wisdom."
– Billy Graham

The book of Proverbs is sometimes referred to as the Book of Wisdom. Solomon, who is considered to be the wisest man who ever lived, wrote much of it. It's interesting that Solomon had 700 wives and 300 concubines. 1 Kings 11 tells the story of how his many pagan wives turned his heart away from God. Because of that, he no longer had the blessings and protection from God.

When we honor God and honor the marriage bed, God will bless us. When we try to do things our own way, we separate ourselves from God. This is a strange thing that God gave Solomon so much wisdom, yet he turned from his own words. He turned from the one thing that God granted him that blessed him beyond any man before or after him.

What this says to me is that every man and every woman is vulnerable to the flesh and we must fight the fight of faith. Don't turn your back on wisdom.

INFLUENCE

In the 1980's, pastor Chuck Swindoll wrote a little book called *Leadership: Influence and Inspiration.* My friend John Maxwell popularized the statement "Leadership is influence. Nothing more. Nothing less." He added to the statement that "you gain influence with others by adding value to them." Everyone has influence in someone else's life. How do you gain a positive influence in someone else's life? We love what (and who) we value.

The late Zig Ziglar said, "You can have everything in life you want, if you will just help enough other people get what they want." When Mr. Ziglar was still with us on the earth, I used to tease him by telling him that he *stole* that from Jesus. Jesus said, "Give and it will be given back to you, pressed down, shaken together and running over." Zig would just rare back and laugh and declare "Well, I know Him personally, so that'll be okay."

When you have influence in someone else's life, you can help them become the person they are created to be. When you take from someone – when you're selfish, you don't help anyone. Not even yourself. You actually take from yourself.

Our culture today teaches us to get what we can. Get all you can. Take from other people. And we are so bound up in our own problems that we can't help others. True joy and fulfillment come from helping others. Give and it will be given to you. It's a spiritual law. It's the *Two Commandments*. When you give time, you'll get time. Maybe not from the same person, but when you help someone, others will help you. When you give money, money will be given back to you.

This is God's design for humanity and community. The reason we have so many problems and need counseling is because we are too focused on ourselves. My wife and I went to a couple of counseling sessions and I came to a very quick conclusion after just two sessions. I came to the conclusion that if I didn't serve my wife and get along with her, I would have to waste more of my time at these boring counseling sessions! I don't have time for that!

My problem wasn't her. It was me. I realized it's a whole lot easier to do it right. I have received the blessing of that decision many times over. I'm still far from perfect, and I'm still a little high maintenance (well, maybe a lot), but I pay my own way. And I make sure my wife's needs are met.

Now I have grandchildren, and I am experiencing a whole other level of love and joy. It puts a comparison perspective on things when I look at how I love my granddaughter, I notice that I am paying attention to every little response. Every little need. Every little detail to make sure she *feels* loved.

My son and my daughter-in-love (I don't like the term *in-law*) lived with us when she was born. She was in my arms every morning. How could you not love something as precious as a little baby? You would have to have a deep hatred for yourself and God to not love a new-born baby.

When you think of the innocence of a newborn baby, you can realize two things...

1. You see how God sees you. Once you are saved, God doesn't see your flaws anymore. They are removed as far as the East is from the West (they never meet). He loves you like that. He treats you like that. Any difficulties you have, just like that newborn baby, come from the fallen state of the world, not from God, unless in some circumstance, He has a loving purpose behind it, like giving His Son to die for us.

2. You can also see what I am seeing with my granddaughter. I think to myself, what if we loved others like I love Gigi? She is three years old at the time of this writing and she is still perfect☺, but when she decides to exercise her own will, and it happens to be against God's ways, I will still love her unconditionally, and I know that love will help her get rec-

onciled to God. I also know that He loves her more than I could ever even imagine.

When all of us get the fact that we can't change anyone but ourselves, we put ourselves in a powerful position of influence. When I change, I open the door for others to change. And the same is true for you.

Why is influence so important?

If no one is following you, you can't lead them. If you want to help people, they have to trust you. You need to have something they want. Something that attracts them to you. That's called influence. It comes through love and respect.

Gaining influence in the world is important too. When you have influence, you can help more people. As a result, you get what you need.

My wife seems to know everyone in Houston. Everyone who knows her, loves her and would do anything for her. The reason? She has sown into so many lives. She is always helping, serving, and giving. She has tremendous influence because she is a giver.

FAITHFULNESS

Trust is the foundation that good relationships are built on. When you are faithful to your spouse, you'll be blessed. I'm not just talking about being faithful sexually. I'm talking about being faithful to God first. Give God the honor and glory due him. Be faithful to your spouse in all areas of life, whatever they may be. Be faithful to your children.

Do what you say you are going to do. Be where you say you are going to be. Don't give your spouse any reason to doubt you. Marriage is about knowing that if all else fails, there's that one person that is always there for you.

I know that about Denise. I know that no matter what happens, she is there for me. I always feel better when I share my problems with her and she shares her wisdom and insight. She has always been faithful to me.

Faithful means being Faith *full*. It means to be *full* of faith! When you are full of faith, you don't worry about things. When you have faith in God, you know He will come through for you. The opposite of faith is fear.

Living in fear creates stress. Being faithful to God gives us the assurance that all will be well. When we know that God is faithful to us because we are full of faith, we don't have to fear.

When you are faithful to your spouse, it gives them comfort that no matter what happens outside the home, there's a refuge inside the home. Before Zig passed away, he wanted to write a book called *The Home Court Advantage.*

When a team plays a home game, they have the advantage of knowing the field of play, of being in their own environment, but most of all, having the support and encouragement of their fans at home.

Be your spouse's biggest fan.

A few months before Zig spoke at my conference, he had fallen down the stairs and was suffering from short-term memory loss, which made him repeat himself over and over.

During the interview on stage, he kept repeating the home court advantage: "The better things are at home, the better things are going to go in the marketplace." After about the sixth time he repeated himself, one of our first-time attendees left the room. I thought because of Zig's condition, he was disappointed.

I peeked out one of the conference room doors and observed that he was on the phone. Okay, maybe he had an emergency phone call. As he began to head back into the large conference room, I stepped out and asked him what happened.

"Zig really got to me." he began. "My girlfriend has been asking me to marry her for over four years. I called her and asked her to marry me!" Even though I questioned the wisdom in proposing over the phone, I was happy that Zig's unintended repetition got to him. They ended up getting married (at our conference) several months later and I got to be the best man.

When you're faithful to your spouse, you open the door for them to be faithful to you. Don't base your level of trustworthiness and faithfulness on what they do or don't do. Think about it this way – if you aren't faithful, how does that encourage them to be?

EXCELLENCE

Proverbs 31 describes an excellent wife...

An excellent wife, who can find? For her worth is far above jewel. The heart of her husband trusts in her. And he will have no lack of gain.[2] She does him good and not evil. All the days of her life.[13]

She looks for wool and flax. And works with her hands in delight.[14] She is like merchant ships; She brings her food from afar.[15] She rises also while it is still night. And gives food to her household. And portions to her maidens.

[16] She considers a field and buys it; From her earnings she plants a vineyard.[17] She girds herself with strength. And makes her arms strong.[18] She senses that her gain is good; Her lamp does not go out at night.

[19] She stretches out her hands to the distaff, And her hands grasp the spindle.[20] She extends her hand to the poor, And she stretches out her hands to the needy.[21] She is not afraid of the snow for her household, For all her household are clothed with scarlet. [22] She makes coverings for herself; Her clothing is fine linen and purple.

[23] Her husband is known in the gates, When he sits among the elders of the land. [24] She makes linen garments and sells them, And supplies belts to the tradesmen.[25] Strength and dignity are her clothing, And she smiles at the future. [26] She opens her mouth in wisdom, And the teaching of kindness is on her tongue.

[27] She looks well to the ways of her household, And does not eat the bread of idleness. [28] Her children rise up and bless her; Her husband also, and he praises her, saying:[29] "Many daughters have done nobly, But you excel them all." [30] Charm is deceitful and beauty is vain, But a woman who fears the Lord, she shall be praised. [31] Give her the product of her hands, And let her works praise her in the gates. -Proverbs 31:10-31

He who finds a wife finds a good thing
And obtains favor from the Lord.
–Proverbs 18:22 (NASB)

Zig said that most people suffer from a poor self-image. We don't understand our value and worth. He said that man is *born to win, designed for accomplishment, engineered for success and endowed with the seeds of greatness.* God created every human being as a special creation. We should treat one another as such.

My business coaching company is named *Phenomenal Products* because I started out selling manuals, CDs, DVDs to help business owners before I got into business coaching as I am today. Bill Beckham, one of my early mentors, came to speak at my conference. He said, "Howard's products are phenomenal, but I'm here to tell you that YOU are the phenomenal product. You are a special creation."

You have tremendous value. You are a phenomenal product.

The Challenge

I don't remember most of my childhood. Outside of certain events, like getting in trouble for stealing bicycles or getting into fights at school, I don't have a lot of memories of bad things happening.

I don't remember being exceptionally happy or sad. My childhood seemed kind of "happy-go-lucky." The sun was shining, I rode my bike. I played softball, basketball and ping-pong at the small civic center at the end of the little dirt road by my house.

Although there were a number of dramatic events in my past, like getting arrested during Spring Break when I was a senior in high school, I don't *feel* those events. I remember my mother and stepfather having to get up in the middle of the night to bail me out of jail, and I remember they weren't very happy about it. But remembering events like that doesn't evoke dramatic emotions for me.

Even though we were poor, I didn't *feel* poor. I knew some people were rich and it seemed weird and uncomfortable being in someone's home that had such nice stuff, but I don't recall feeling any dramatically negative emotions about it.

Realizing that I don't remember a lot of emotion growing up, my assumption is that I've probably stuffed a lot of it away somewhere. All of life's experiences are recorded somewhere in our soul and manifest in one-way or another. Perhaps one of the reasons I didn't emote negatively was due to one of the unwritten rules in our family: We never "crossed" one another.

Healthy conflict didn't exist. If we disagreed, we just got kept it to ourselves. We withdrew. We didn't argue. We each went our own way and did our own thing.

After I moved to Houston to live with my biological father and his wife, they would sometimes give me advice. Usually related to my business. I would listen very carefully, but often wouldn't use the advice. Many times, I would end up doing it my own way.

One day my stepmother Marie frustratingly said, "Howard is the best listener you'll *ever* find, but then he turns around and does exactly what *he* wants to do!"

At some point during my marriage, I realized that Italians from New Jersey practice healthy conflict on a regular basis. With my upbringing, I thought if you yelled and screamed at one other, that it meant you *hated* each other, but that obviously was not the case with Italians from Jersey. Denise and I would have a disagreement and she would come out swinging; verbally of course. Here lips were moving 90 miles an hour and her hands were flying.

Psychologists call this "fight or flight". Denise was a fighter and I was a flighter. She would start fighting and I immediately withdrew, which sent her into even more of a tizzy.

The reason? When an Italian stops talking, you know you've crossed the line. If an Italian isn't talking, they have probably been offended. Not realizing this, I went quiet without knowing the argument hadn't even warmed up yet!

Now, please understand that neither of us was aware this was happening, but once I became aware of how we were communicating, I began to argue my case instead of just withdrawing. We had a better outcome as a result. Then, I found that if I could make her laugh, it would be even better!

After 37 years of marriage, we don't really argue. We might debate a subject, or see things differently, but we don't have arguments like we used to. There are a couple of reasons for this. One, is that we have both matured. Second, fear is not driving emotions. When you lack faith, your subconscious fears can go crazy on you. Finally, we just understand each other better.

All of life is about relationships. And relationships are built on healthy communication. We are all wired differently and we all communicate differently. Each of us has different values about things like money, time, vacations, dreams, children, other people, the world, and God. In other words, we might have different values about almost everything!

When Denise and I got together, she was attracted to me because "I had potential".

On one of our many trips, we shared a big mansion on the beach with several other couples in Belize.

She *still* says I have room to grow. At the big dinner table at the mansion on the beach in Belize, as we went around the table sharing what we liked most about our spouses, Denise said, "He has potential." What? We had been married for *thirty-one* years at the time.

I have *potential*?

The more I thought about it, the more I liked her response. Even though she meant it to be cute and witty, she knows I haven't even gotten warmed up yet. I've done a lot of things in my life, but I feel like I haven't even gotten started. She knows there's another level. She can see that God isn't nearly done with me yet.

And that is true for you as well. No matter what you have done - no matter what God has done in your life thus far, He wants to do a *new* work in you today. A *new* work in your marriage. A *new* work in your relationships. A *new* work in your career.

My definition of success is becoming the person God created you to be. Learning to love God and love others is a journey to help us discover who we are, where we are, and where we are going.

Having a strong relationship with God and others, helps us flesh that out. Jesus was the ultimate expression of "God with skin on". Your life and your relationships help you discover your phenomenal potential. To help you *become* the person you are destined to become. We all need one another to for support, encouragement and accountability to grow to our full potential.

You may not be getting that right now. That's okay. Provide it to others anyway. *You* be the person you want the other person to be. You may not be able to change another person, but if you are willing to change, you open the door for the other person. You may be in a difficult situation right now. Maybe really bad things are happening.

Don't lose hope.

Trust God and love others.

Relationships are based on trust and communication and even though we love and trust one another, many times we fail to communicate. Everyone is wired differently and we all have different values and we all communicate differently.

One of the most helpful tools for myself and our coaching community is the Positive Personality Profiles by Dr. Robert Rohm. Discover your unique profile at www.howardpartridge.com/disc

An accurate personality assessment that has been validated can help dramatically improve relationships in any setting whether that be a family or a team. Since the free report will share what you need to know, I won't take the time to outline the human behavior model here, but do yourself a favor, and download that free report.

Then, get an assessment for your yourself, your spouse, your children and your team members. Anyone you have a close relationship with or that you work with on a regular basis should do an assessment.

Why? Because there are 41 different communication styles! It's a simple, easy assessment that can change your life. One of my coaching clients was having difficulty in her marriage. Her and her husband were separated actually.

Their only daughter, who was five years old at the time, turned from a lovely, positive, bright-smiling child to a sad countenance, and she went from making wonderful grades at school, to getting in trouble. My client was mean to her staff which created a good deal of unnecessary stress in the office.

When Alyse learned this model and began to use it, everything changed. Her and her husband are back together, and the family is whole again. Recently, I did my very first "family dream day". Normally, I meet with the business owner to help them understand where they are in their business career and how to get clarity on their vision.

Alyse asked me if she could bring the family, so they could talk about family dreams. "Of course!" was my enthusiastic response! We talked about vacations, school, career, communication in the family, and more. Their family is gelling because they learned to *communicate* with one another.

Also, Alyse learned how to communicate with her staff more effectively.

She learned that she is task-oriented, which means the *people* side of the equation was being ignored. Today her team is rocking! In fact, they are practically running her business *for* her and they have a phenomenal relationship.

Go to www.howardpartridge.com/disc to download a free report on personality styles.

Voice Texting?

Today's technology can present communication problems as well. If you've ever sent a voice text, you know what I mean! In fact, relying on technology to communicate is not your best option. There are too many opportunities for miscommunication which end up offending someone.

I follow business owner groups on Facebook and many of the newbie business owners post screen shots of their customer's text messages, usually dealing with some kind of a conflict, whether it be pricing or a follow up request.

They are asking others in the group how to respond. The others in the group are most likely newbies themselves, and have no skin in the game, so they give really bad advice. "You should say this..." their advice typically starts out. Or "what I would say is..."

How about this instead... "pick up the phone and *call* them!" You think exchanging text messages, or worse, social media posts are going to solve the problem? Not a chance. Pick up the phone and talk to them. Both parties will have less stress and it will lessen the chance for one of you to say something hurtful.

Speaking of that, why do couples have fights via text? Pick... up... the... telephone! And even better, wait until you can meet in person!

Folks, this isn't that complicated! If we are not careful, any of us can fall into this trap. If you understand that all of these conflicts come from a place of fear, which comes from fleshly desires, you will get along better. Humble yourself.

Jesus' brother James talks about this in the *Book of James*...

What is the source of quarrels and conflicts among you? Is the source not your pleasures that wage war in your body's parts? You lust and do not have, so you commit murder. And you are envious and cannot obtain, so you fight and quarrel.

You do not have because you do not ask. You ask and do not receive, because you ask with the wrong motives, so that you may spend what you request on your pleasures. You adulteresses, do you not know that friendship with the world is hostility toward God?

Therefore, whoever wants to be a friend of the world makes himself an enemy of God. Or do you think that the Scripture says to no purpose, "He jealously desires the Spirit whom He has made to dwell in us"? But He gives a greater grace. Therefore, it says, "God is opposed to the proud, but gives grace to the humble." Submit therefore to God. But resist the devil, and he will flee from you. Come close to God and He will come close to you. Cleanse your hands, you sinners; and purify your hearts, you double-minded. Be miserable, and mourn, and weep; let your laughter be turned into mourning, and your joy into gloom. Humble yourselves in the presence of the Lord, and He will exalt you. (James 4:1-10)

God wants us to discover our unique purpose for being here. Many marriages get started the wrong way. We don't get married for the right reasons, and we don't really understand what marriage is all about, and before too long our differences in opinion, in tastes, and how to resolve issues gets us thinking we married the wrong person.

Since you're committed for life (aren't you?), life will be a lot better if you begin to understand your mate and understand yourself better. Although Denise and I have many common interests, there are many ways we couldn't be more different.

If you aren't committed for life, this book will be useless to you. You must understand the *benefit* of committing for life. The benefit, is you'll become the person you were created to be. Dealing with others may seem like sandpaper for a while, but once the work is done, you'll have a soft, smooth product. Make a decision to commit for life. Make a commitment to the covenant relationship God has established.

What I've found is that when you begin to understand the gifts of your spouse, you'll have more joy and meaning in your marriage. Where would I be if Denise wasn't good with money? When you value one another for who God created them to be, even if they haven't matured yet, everything changes for the better.

How we see and value one another is the key. All humans are phenomenal products. God don't make no junk! When you begin to understand that *you* are a phenomenal product. That *you* are born to win – that *you* were designed for accomplishment, engineered for success and endowed with the seeds of greatness as Zig Ziglar said – and you begin to understand that *everyone* is made that way, you begin to see that everyone has a gift and a calling.

Marriage is about developing that gift and calling. You may feel that your spouse isn't helping you develop your gift and calling. You may feel they are actually keeping you from it. Even if that is true, trust God.

He knows the very number of hairs on your head. Jesus said a sparrow doesn't fall to the ground without God knowing about it. Do you believe it? If you will simply *trust God* and *love others* instead of being selfish, your life will change. Your marriage then has a chance of getting better.

Please understand that if your spouse is mentally ill, you'll need professional help to deal with that. This is not a counseling book. I'm not a therapist or a counselor. I'm just a regular guy appealing to the good and godly conscious of fellow believers in Jesus Christ.

By the way, be sure to pick up a copy of Zig Ziglar's book *Courtship After Marriage*.
"Many marriages would be better if the husband and wife clearly understood they are on the same side." – Zig Ziglar

Oranges and legless people

Every person on the planet has a unique calling, a unique background, and a unique personality style.

A while back, my friend Kirby Lammers taught me an exercise using oranges, which reveals how unique humans are, even though in many ways we are the same. In a group setting, get about a dozen oranges of the same type. Have people in the audience come up and pick out an orange.

Have them study the orange very carefully for a few minutes, and then hand it back in. Mix them up and wait about thirty minutes or until the meeting is almost over. Then invite them to come up and pick out their orange. My experience has been that each and every one will find their orange.

Here's why...

Although every orange looks the same from a distance, each one is unique. Each one has slightly different physical attributes. Some have scars and look like they have been through a lot. Some are still green in some areas. Some look so perfect, you would think they are plastic. Some have freckles. Some have a slightly different color than the others.

Isn't that like humans? From a distance, we mostly look the same. We have a head, a body, and some of us have hands and feet! I know of two men who don't have legs, and one of them has no arms. The other has one arm and a finger! They are both ironically named Nick. I've never met Nick Vujicic, but I have spent some time with Nick Santonastosso.

You don't have to get close to them to see the difference in the outward appearance, but most people have the same body parts. We have similar physical attributes. The closer you get to another human, you find that many of us have scars. We are a little green in some areas. We are different colors. Some of us look a little plastic on the outside. Some of us look a little banged up. The question is what's on the inside? When you peel an orange, you might find that the beautiful one is sour on the inside. Or one that has major scars on the outside is sweet on the inside.

The point is that every human has a unique fingerprint, and a unique past that has created the person you see today. In order to become the person we are called to be, we have to become aware of our worth and recognize that in others. And we have to understand the other person's difference, especially our spouses!

When we begin to understand that we all have a unique gift, a unique past, and a unique personality style, we can understand why that person doesn't think like we think, and doesn't act like we do.

What language do you speak?

In 1995 Gary Chapman wrote a book called *The Five Love Languages: How to Express Heartfelt Commitment to Your Mate.* It outlines five ways to express and experience love that Chapman calls "love languages": gifts, quality time, words of affirmation, acts of service, and physical touch.

Chapman shares that emotionally people need to receive love and uses the metaphor of a 'love tank' to explain people's need to be loved. He also writes that people should not use the love languages that they like the most but rather the love languages that their loved ones can receive.

Each person has one primary and one secondary love language. He suggests that to discover a love language, one must observe the way he or she expresses love to others, analyze what he complains about most often, and what he requests from his significant other most often.

People tend to naturally give love in the way that they prefer to receive love. My love language is words of affirmation. I crave affirmation and appreciation. I need those that love me to *tell* me! I'm so appreciative of those that do. When they tell me how they feel about me, my love tank gets filled up and I'm fueled and ready to take on the world. When I don't get that, I don't feel good. My second love language is physical touch. I'm a hugger. I need that. Since we all tend to give love the way we receive love, I tend to love Denise that way. To be sweet and kind to her. Denise on the other hand prefers acts of service. I remind myself of that and do little things around the house, and that communicates love to her. It may be a small thing, like doing the dishes every day, or cleaning the house, but it means something to her. Her secondary love language is gifts. And she gives love that way. She is always giving gifts and serving people.

Recognizing your spouse's love language, and using it, shows that you care. Many times, it is the first step that needs to be taken to begin improving a relationship. To simply begin operating in their love language. As I shared earlier, when I first got saved, I wanted Denise to know the truth, so I told her what the bible said often. Maybe a little *too* often. That didn't work for her.

But when I began to love her in her love language by taking out the garbage and doing things around the house to serve her, she began to accept some of the things I had to share. A pastor recently told me, "Truth without love is brutal. Love without truth is sentimental." When you communicate in their love language rather than yours, you will have a better chance of connecting.

Chapter 5

The Five Secrets of Phenomenal YOU+H

I recently wrote a book called *Phenomenal You+H – The 7 Lies Between You and Success.* In that book, I share that according to Mr. Ziglar, everyone wants the same nine things out of life.

Having invested the past ten years helping carry on the legacy of Zig Ziglar, I have studied his material extensively. I have personally reviewed thousands of hours of Ziglar content and invested as many hours sharing it with others.

Currently I serve as VP of Training Operations for Ziglar and was blessed to be the very first Ziglar Legacy Certified Trainer, thanks to Tom Ziglar.

For most of the ten years I have been involved, I have learned from Mr. Ziglar that there are *eight* things everyone wants out of life…

To be happy
To be healthy
To be at least reasonably prosperous
To have friends
To have peace of mind
To have good family relationships
To feel secure
To have hope for the future

But recently, Nightingale Conant came out with a book called *A View from*

the Top, which was in essence a transcript from the audio recordings with the same name. In this book, it had *nine* things listed instead of eight. The ninth one is…
"To love and to be loved."

I don't know the back story of how that one got added, but I'm so glad it was added. There's a lengthy story behind why I wrote *Phenomenal You+H* that I won't retell here. The short story is God gave me a vision for young people and I'm just following His lead.

It turns out that I love kids! I love their energy, their creativity, their joy and excitement. But what happens to kids in our culture? Before too long, their bright eyes go dull. Their excitement turns to boredom. Like Adam and Eve, their innocence is taken from them by the "knowledge of evil".

Our young people are desperate for love. The break-down of family values in our society has crippled our kids. Like everyone else, they want those nine things, especially the last one.

The problem is they are going about it the wrong way. They are listening to the wrong voices. They are being lied to. I'll let you read the book for yourself, and please get a copy for every kid you know.

For now, let's discover five secrets of our Phenomenal You+H

You. When kids understand that they were created by a loving God, that has a plan and a purpose for their life, they will make better choices. When we believe the lie, that we just evolved from animals, we basically feel like we are the result of a cosmic accident! *Phenomenal You+H* starts with YOU. You are phenomenal, and when you add His Love, His sacrifice to the equation, you get You plus Him = Phenomenal Success.

Others. Mr. Ziglar said "you can have everything in life you want (all nine of those things), if you will help enough Other people get what they want. What if our kids really learned to serve others? I think they would learn something about love.

Understanding. Our young people are experiencing an identity crisis and they are going to great lengths to show it off. They don't understand who they are and whose they are, therefore they don't feel understood. Maybe we could learn how to be a little less religious and a little more relational toward them.

+ The plus sign is the symbol of the cross of Jesus Christ. Scripture says the cross is the only thing that can reconcile us to our loving God. The amazing Love that God bestowed upon us is the missing link to true success in life, and the key to understanding forgiveness and unconditional love.

Him. Scripture reveals that Christ *in* you is the hope of glory. We can only love like God loves by allowing Him to live through us as the second chapter of Galatians talks about.

Finally, another book you'll want to grab is *Raising Positive Kids in a Negative World* by Zig Ziglar.

"Our children are our only hope for the future. We are their only hope for now and the future." – Zig Ziglar

"To a child, LOVE is spelled T-I-M-E" – Zig Ziglar

Chapter 6

The Six Secrets of a Phenomenal F.A.M.I.L.Y.

I'm originally from L.A. (Lower Alabama!) I grew up on welfare in Alabama. There were seven kids crammed into a six hundred square foot house. The roof on that house was so bad, we had to get out all the pots and pans to catch the leaks. My mother fed us on a hundred dollars a month from the welfare department. My biological father left the five kids at that time behind when I was only a year old. I only met him twice in my life.

When you grow up in an environment like that, what are you likely to turn out like? For me, it was a rebellious teenager. I got kicked out of the house by my stepdad before I was even eighteen years old. I always have to acknowledge that my stepdad took on seven kids and got us off welfare, but I was a lot to handle. I deserved what I got.

The next night after getting kicked out, I climbed on a Greyhound bus to Houston, TX with twenty-five *cents* in my pocket. My sister was living with my real dad and his new wife, and I was ready for a change. My dad and I became very close and I became close to his new family. And I still love my family back home.

Denise and I only have one son, Christian. He is a great dad and husband to our daughter-in-love Susy. They blessed us with two precious grandchildren so far. Gianna and Elijah.

Having the "kids" (as I refer to all four of them) close by is a real blessing. As

Christian was growing up, I was gone a lot. I worked a lot and I traveled a lot. As a result, Christian and I had a rough time over the years. Today, even though we don't always understand each other, we love each other. We are committed to our relationship by continuing to work on it.

Now that he has a family, and they live close by it gives us an opportunity to spend time with him, Susy and the kids. I get the opportunity to love our grandkids and help them to understand who they are and *whose* they are. I get to lead and guide them. I want them to be as whole as they can possibly be.

Neither Christian or myself really had grandparents that we were close to. My grandmother died before I was even born. My mother lives in Alabama, we live in Texas. Denise's parents lived in New Jersey before coming to Houston for the last three years of their life. Christian was able to spend a lot of time with them then, but at that point, they were in their late eighties.

Susy's parents live close by also, as well. The result is that our grandkids have lots of love and support close by. A recipe for a great foundation. Christian and Susy work with me in one of the "family" businesses, so it creates a very close relationship and bond.

They love God and are drawing closer to Him every single day, and I do have to say, there is nothing like the love and joy of grandkids! That is another level of love that is beyond phenomenal! Especially when they are as cute as ours are!

You've heard the old sayings about grandchildren, right? Like "If I had known they were going to be this much fun, I would have been nicer to their parents!" Or, "If I had of known having grandkids was gonna be so good, I would've had them first!"

I don't know who is more obnoxious, someone who just got into multi-level marketing, or a new grandparent! You know what happens when someone gets into multi-level marketing right? They are convinced their product will solve all the world's problems and they pester their friends and family to the point of finally giving in and buying the product so they will just leave you alone!

And new grandparents aren't any better. They have to show off pictures of their grandchild to everyone they meet. That's all they talk about! When I found out Christian and Susy were expecting, I made a decision that I wouldn't be like that as a grandparent. And I'm not. I'm worse!

Family Values

You know what you value by what you do. How you spend your time and money. Values are the standards you live by. Values dictate your conduct as a team. In my work as a business coach, we encourage companies to establish what I call their M.V.P. (Mission, Values and Purpose). Mission is what we do every day. For example, *we deliver the most phenomenal service experience every day.* It's the "what" we do.

Purpose is why we do it. For example: *To help people have more freedom in their life.* It's why we exist.

Values are *who* we are. Or who we want to become. We may not be there yet, but it's who we aspire to be as a team. In this case as a family.

Values support the what and the why. They determine our conduct. Ultimately, they determine how we love each other.

I have a client who owns a large company. Their values spell out FAMILY. I think their values would work for any family, so I have listed their values below followed by my notes.

F - **Focus**. *We are focused on the things that matter.*

What matters in *your* family? Do you have a set of family values? Jeff Dudan, a collaborator on a new project I am working on, has their family values written down. I'm sure they have them posted in their home somewhere as well.

A - **Adaptability**. *We are flexible and collaborative, always keeping the end result in mind.*

Wouldn't we all get along better if we were a little less rigid. In other words, seek to understand before being understood. Could we get along better if we were a little more collaborative instead of competitive?

Keeping the end result in mind is what it is all about. What outcome do you want in a relationship? Remember, love is not offended. If you die to yourself, you don't feel anything. As one of my pastor friends often said "Dead people don't feel anything."

M - Morality. *We operate at the highest moral standards.*

Can we agree that immorality is selfish? God warns us about immorality, not because He wants to control us, but because He loves us! He wants the best for us! I will always remember a presentation by my friend Dr. Robert Rohm on the Ten Commandments. We always have a Spiritual Session at our conferences to honor God and to share the good news. I would be remiss if I held a conference on success and left out the most important ingredient: A relationship with God! Dr. Rohm shared the reasons behind the Ten Commandments. Space doesn't allow me to share the entire message here, but he pointed out that the commandments were to help the nation of Israel and its people thrive.

I - Intentionality. *We are aggressively intentional, determined, passionate, disciplined, dedicated and relentless in every pursuit, every day.*

Isn't this a wonderful way to live your life? Leadership expert, John Maxwell wrote a book called *Intentional Living.* At the time he wrote it, I was involved in his highest-level programs. He told us that book was his most important book.

The world's top leadership expert understands the value of intention. Our intentions are a result of our motives. What are your motives when it comes to your family? What intentions do you have? Will you live intentionally or just let life happen to you? *Passionate, determination, disciplined and dedicated* are all words that would describe a person who loves (who is committed to another).

L - Leadership. *We lead by example with humility, through relationship, honesty and boldness.*

In 1985 Pastor Chuck Swindoll wrote a book called *Leadership: Influence that Inspires.* John Maxwell popularized the definition of leadership as "Leadership is influence. Nothing more. Nothing less." And how do you gain influence in someone else's life? By adding *value* to them.

Zig Ziglar said "You can have everything in life you want, if you will just help enough other people get what they want." That's love. That's leadership. That's leading your family with love. Humility, relationship, and honesty. That's love! Do we need to be bold some time? Yes. Sometimes we need to practice tough love.

Y - Yearning. *We yearn to serve, to inspire and to supersede our mission and goals.*

Serve! Yes! That's love! If you want to inspire someone serve them! People think inspiration comes from a motivational speech or being positive all the time. It can, but if you want to really inspire someone, serve them.

Scripture tells us to "love our enemies. And when we do, we will heap burning coals upon their head." What in the world does *that* mean? It means they will be ashamed of how they treated you. Remember, don't return evil for evil. Return good all the time, even when it is difficult. Remember our example? Jesus Christ on the cross? Not fun. Not pretty. But powerful.

Supersede our mission and goals. When we allow God to love through us, we can do that. "Unto Him who will do exceedingly, abundantly more than we could ever think or imagine" Scripture says. Wow, that's a lot. I can think and imagine a great deal. And He will do even more! Isn't that exciting?

Chapter 7

The Seven Secrets of a Phenomenal HUSBAND

One of my coaching clients, John Michalidis (MICK-EH-LEE-DIS), is a tall, outspoken, loud, boisterous man. A licensed attorney and a licensed real estate broker. Obviously super smart. And if you didn't know him, you would assume that he was arrogant by his gregarious nature.

Like many people, I was a little taken back by this outspoken character. But the more I got to know John, the more I realized that he also has a huge, tender heart. I was in Florida once and he took me to see a ministry he supports that helps troubled youth. Then I learned about several other ministries he is involved in that he not only supports financially, but also with his time.

Once I got to know John, I found out that he's a big "teddy bear". I absolutely love being with him and he is so funny. When I get close to someone, I often give them a nickname. *Cheesecake* became John's nickname because of a story he told me one night at a get together after a seminar.

He told me that when he was a kid, just before Thanksgiving one year, that his mother had a store-bought cheesecake in the refrigerator. Thanksgiving Day was a couple of days away, but he really wanted some of that cheesecake!

He slid the cheesecake out of the box and studied it to see how he might get a piece of it without anyone knowing it. He gently turned the cheesecake over, and peeled back the cardboard base. He then took a spoonful of the cheesecake out of the bottom. He then replaced the cardboard base, put it back in the box and back in the fridge. Brilliant! No one will ever know!

But then, he wanted another piece. He went through the entire procedure again. Carefully remove it from the box without damaging it, gently remove the cardboard and take another spoonful.

So far so good.

Then, he wanted another piece! And another. And another. By the time he got done "tasting" the cheesecake, there was a giant crater in the bottom of it, but it still looked good on the top!

Until...

His mom removed it from the refrigerator Thanksgiving morning. It had imploded. The next thing he heard was "Johnny!!!!!"

I tell you this story so you get a sense of John's humor. The next thing I learned about Cheesecake is that he wasn't married. He had never been married. And he wasn't in his twenties or thirties. Based on his personality, you know whoever might marry him has to be a special woman. Plus, at his age, who are you going to find?

Well, God is in the miracle business. John found someone. Linda is the sweetest, kindest, most gentle, loving person you could ever meet. They decided to get married, and asked me to be the best man. I was honored.

By that time, I had learned the secrets of a phenomenal WIFE, but I didn't have anything for the HUSBAND. So, in my speech at the reception, I shared the Four Secrets of a Phenomenal WIFE and created the 7 Secrets of a Phenomenal HUSBAND.

This piece is dedicated to Cheesecake...

Again, this is not just for husbands, but all of us.

A Phenomenal Husband is...

Humble
Understanding
Supportive
Brave
Available
Nurturing
Determined

HUMBLE

But a humble spirit will obtain honor.
Proverbs 29:23b

The last thing an American male would be accused of is being humble. A better description would be arrogant, selfish, and maybe even be a jerk. Even men in the church! The reason is that the American media has shaped our culture rather than the Church.

The media portrays men to be intimidating, nasty, and absolutely sinful, or stupid and lazy. Even worse is that some men are living up to it because Arts & Entertainment has more influence than Church and Community.

In today's culture, if you aren't pompous and arrogant, you aren't considered a man.

The result is an overworked, self-loathing (truth be told), stressed-out man trying to display his manliness through sports stats and world affairs. But does that match the image that God has for men? Do you have to be "macho" to be powerful?

What if you could be powerful without being arrogant? What if you could be Godly without being a pansy?

As I was thinking about the letters in the word husband, I picked Humble for the letter H. After that, I got to thinking about Honor. Then I found this verse...

Before destruction the heart of man is haughty, But humility goes before honor. – Proverbs 18:12

Again, Zig Ziglar said, "The chief cause of failure and unhappiness is trading what you want most for what you want now."

What do you really want most? You want to honor God and be accepted by Him. You want to have favor with others. How do you break out of the negativity that is all around you and become the man you want to be, so you can be the husband you want to be?

Humble yourself before God. Don't try to be the man the world wants you to be. Who cares what your worthless buddies think? Who cares what people who are going straight to hell think? Is that too harsh?

When you humble yourself by being the man God wants you to be, you'll be blessed with riches, honor, and life. That doesn't mean that your 401k will go up. Riches mean you will have a rich relationship with God. He will always take care of your needs. Walking in faith is knowing and understanding that God cares about you and will take care of your every need.

Being humble doesn't mean that you have no power. Just the opposite. Now you have God's power. It doesn't mean that you aren't bold. Jesus was as bold as a lion. In meekness we have power. When we are weak, He is strong.

What does that look like in daily life? Treating others with respect. Not demanding that you be preferred over other people. When you do that, God will exalt you to a high place and give you tremendous favor.

Did you know that the reason men are cocky is because deep down they're afraid? They have a poor self-image and they are trying to compensate for it. Fear drives that. Understand that you are made in God's image. As a Christian, you have not been given a spirit of fear, but of power and love and a sound mind.

You have been set free from having to play the part of the all-powerful American male. You no longer have to pretend to be something you're not. Just accept who you are in Christ and walk in that.

It also doesn't mean you have to be ashamed of being blessed.

The fear of the Lord is the instruction for wisdom. And before honor *comes* humility. -Proverbs 15:33

UNDERSTANDING

In his best-selling book, *The 7 Habits of Highly Effective People*, Stephen R. Covey encouraged us to "seek to understand before being understood".

The natural result of being born into original sin means that we come into the world selfish. This is the paradox. On one hand, we are made in God's image, we are "born to win" as Zig said. We are a "phenomenal product", a special creation. But because of the fall of man, we are born selfish.

Dr. Bill Gillham says we are spiritually "still-born". We are fleshly. We only think of ourselves. We don't learn to be selfish. We already are. We have to *un*learn that. We have to learn not to be selfish. This entire book is about being unselfish in our relationships. That's the key to a healthy relationship.

Understanding others is a start in the right direction. Seek to understand where the other person is coming from rather than focusing on your own feelings and needs. This is exactly what Jesus did...

Scripture instructs us...

Therefore, if there is any encouragement in Christ, if there is any consolation of love, if there is any fellowship of the Spirit, if any affection and compassion, make my joy complete by being of the same mind, maintaining the same love, united in spirit, intent on one purpose.

Do nothing from selfishness or empty conceit, but with humility of mind regard one another as more important than yourselves; do not merely look out for your own personal interests, but also for the interests of others. Have this attitude in yourselves which was also in Christ Jesus, who, although He existed in the form of God, did not regard equality with God a thing to be grasped, but emptied Himself, taking the form of a bond-servant, and being made in the likeness of men.

Being found in appearance as a man, He humbled Himself by becoming obedient to the point of death, even death on a cross. For this reason also, ***God highly exalted Him****, and bestowed on Him the name which is above every name, so that at the name of Jesus every knee will bow, of those who are in heaven and on earth and under the earth, and that every tongue will confess that Jesus Christ is Lord, to the glory of God the Father.* - Philippians 2:1-10"

Wow, did you notice that this passage said, "For this reason also, God highly exalted Him"? When you seek God's will for your life, He will bless you. He will bless your marriage. He will bless your life. How can we expect to be selfish and do our own will and still be blessed? Jesus, who existed in the form of God, humbled Himself and then He was exalted.

Once when my son had a little spat with his wife, the two of them were going back and forth about who did what and who said what. He was upset and frustrated. He asked me for advice, and I simply shared what I am sharing with you now.

I encouraged him to focus on understanding her and where she was coming from. Try to understand how she feels. I told him that a "dead man" has no feelings. In other words, when you die to the flesh, no one can hurt you. No one could hurt Jesus, because He knew who He was and Whose He was.

When you know who *you* are, that you are created in God's image, and *whose* you are, that you have the Holy Spirit of God inside of you, then you understand that you have nothing to prove. You begin to *love* others rather than satisfy yourself.

When you do that, you actually get what it is you were after in the first place, which is joy and fulfillment. Empty yourself and try to understand where your significant other is coming from. Maybe they have tremendous problems. Help them. Maybe they have tremendous hurts. Comfort them.

Maybe they are angry and selfish. Be the person that can take it like Jesus did.

I *know* that deep down you want to be that man, but you're afraid to be that person because you think it will cost you the things that are dear to you. You think you are missing out on all the exciting stuff the world has to offer.

Listen to the Apostle John who Jesus loved:

> *Do not love the world nor the things in the world. If anyone loves the world, the love of the Father is not in him. For all that is in the world, the lust of the flesh and the lust of the eyes and the boastful pride of life, is not from the Father, but is from the world. The world is passing away, and also its lusts; but the one who does the will of God lives forever.* – 1 John 2:15-17

SUPPORTIVE

Earlier, I talked about the four different personality styles D, I, S, C. The way you're wired and the way you're brought up have a great deal to do with how you interact with your significant other.

I'm a high D, which is Outgoing and Task Oriented, and I learned from my mother to just hunker down and get the job done. That, along with the natural selfishness humans have when void of the Holy Spirit or when we choose not to operate in the Spirit, I make long lists of things to do and have it all planned out. Every minute of the hour is planned of what I'm going to do.

The only problem is that I haven't left room for the needs of others. Like my wife. Then, she wants me to do something for her. Something that doesn't seem nearly as important as the tasks on my list. Have you ever experienced that?

My wife is an I/S which means she is very PEOPLE oriented. She is very supportive and interactive. Another factor that comes into play is Gary Chapman's love language. Hers is "acts of service". She serves that way, and she wants to be loved that way.

Brave

When I first wrote this manuscript six years ago, and when I shared at John and Linda's wedding, I put BOLD as the word here, but recently a friend of mine sent me a text message that caused me to change it to BRAVE.

He is starting a marriage coaching program for men (can I get a Hallelujah ladies?). He asked me whether it should be called *The Bold Husband* or *The Brave Husband.* I immediately replied with "brave" because it better describes the posture needed from men. Plus, being brave includes being bold, but not arrogant.

Every woman wants the man in her life to be brave. To face the danger for her. This is the proper order of things. This is the way God set things up, so it doesn't matter what culture says.

Available

The CEO of a very large company that I did a lot of work with made it very clear early in our relationship that he wouldn't interrupt our meetings with an incoming call, unless it was his wife. He worked a lot and was very successful, but made a commitment to his wife that no matter what he was doing, he would take her call. And over many years of doing business with him before he sold the company for untold millions, he kept that promise as far as I could see.

Someone once said "no amount of business success can compensate for failure at home". That's wise advice. I can't say I do as well as he did, but I'm thankful for text messaging, so Denise can let me know if something is urgent. I'm also thankful that Denise is pretty independent.

Either party in a relationship needs to be considerate of the other person's responsibilities and give them the space they need. Every personality type has different needs, so you have to work out how much is too much and how much is too little, but the point is that when you love someone, you are available to them. If you love God, be available. If you love your spouse, be available. If you love your kids, be available.

Obviously, you cannot be available to everyone all the time, but if the person you love needed you in the middle of the night, you would be there for them.

This is an area that I am still working on myself. As I write this, I realize this book is as much for me as it is you. And if my wife reads this, you may hear an audible "AMEN!"

Nice

Why is it that we are super nice to strangers, but not so much to those who are closest to us? For example, when your cell phone rings and you don't know who it is, you're likely to answer with a very pleasant tone. But when your spouse calls, they get a short "hey" or a gruff "hello".

My right-hand man, Santiago Arango who is a phenomenal husband answers his wife's call with "Hi honey, I'm crazy about you!". Wow, that sounds a little over the top, but that statement would surely diffuse just about any negative situation, wouldn't it?

And that's the point of being nice. I read a story once about a salesperson who called on a big account. He was rude to everyone in the building not realizing it would come back to the buyer.

Of course, he didn't make the sale.

There is no reason, and no benefit of being rude to others. And that's the point. Outcome. What kind of *outcome* do want in your relationships?

Love is not offended. Love suffers no wrong, so it doesn't matter if someone is rude to you. Don't return evil for evil.

Determined

A phenomenal husband doesn't give up. Everyone appreciates someone who doesn't waver in the face of opposition. Perseverance through trials creates character. Whether you are a man or woman, husband or wife, father or mother, brother or sister, son or daughter, develop an unwavering spirit. Grit will get you through the tough times.

Chapter 8

The Eight Secrets of a Phenomenal Marriage

As you can clearly see by now, I love acronyms. It makes things easier for me to remember; and I guess they help me to remember how to spell things too. At the dinner table in Belize, I asked for help putting words to the letters of the word "marriage". I began, "M – A – R – R – A – "That's when my friend Bruce interrupted me by clearing his throat first, "Uhm... Howard, I think if you are going to write a book on marriage, you should know how to spell the word first!"

We all got a big laugh out of it. Two things I've learned doing seminars: Don't do math in my head (or on my fingers) on stage, and don't try and spell something without a PowerPoint slide or help from the audience!

Anyway, here's what we came up with for marriage:

Mature – A mature spouse is responsible. Following along with our theme of being in a covenant for life – for better or worse – in sickness and health – till death do us part – we must kill the immaturity that causes us so much trouble.

Immaturity causes major stress in the marriage. Some of us just need to grow up. It's a big responsibility to be married. It's a big deal to actually practice Phenomenal Love. This is the reason that so many marriages end up on the rocks. We have the wrong idea about what marriage is. We listen to Hollywood rather than God. We have in our mind that we should be able to do what we want, when we want, and that everyone should be fine with it.

We receive affection and meaning from other people, other sources, and we become immature and irresponsible with those relationships. We have hobbies. For some husbands, it might be hunting or fishing. He thinks he should be able to go hunting whenever he wants regardless of the responsibilities at home. Guys are like that. Their hobby, their business, and their projects are important to them.

I have a friend whose wife has a spending problem. Credit cards were maxed out; they were paying huge interest rates and late fees. It cost them their marriage. She was too proud to get help. I've been there myself. Fortunately, Denise is wise with money.

My marriage suffered because I was immature. One of the reasons I married Denise was because she was not only stable, but she was mature. I evaded responsibility. I wanted to do my own thing. Fortunately for me, Denise is a strong, independent woman and today we have a phenomenal relationship and are blessed financially.

We must realize that no amount of pleasure, no amount of business success, and no amount of recognition or affection can compensate for failure at home. I remember two occasions when I had to "man up" and make an intentional decision to put my wife first.

The first occasion had to do with the ministry I spoke about earlier in this book. After two years of refusing to go to church, Denise started taking Christian to the Baptist church in our neighborhood. I wouldn't go. I was too prideful. One day God spoke to me and I heard something like, "My Son sat in synagogues that didn't glorify me. Who do you think you are?"

I was willing to humble myself and began going to that church. I sat there with my arms crossed and a frown on my face. The church seemed to be everything I didn't like about church. Then a miracle happened. There was a split in the church!

The new pastor believed in community and preached the Word of God. He has empowered people in the church to *belong*. We have been at the church now for over two decades! Denise and I sit on the front row, and stand with our hands raised high during worship.

It was during those "dark" days that my brother and his wife got a hold of me. Thank God for people who love you enough to tell you the *truth*!

I later realized that my calling was not that ministry. My calling is to do what I'm doing now. I didn't realize it at the time, but the training I got from that ministry prepared me for what I am doing now, and I will always be grateful for my mentors. I still see one of them often and he continues to encourage me in what I am doing.

The point is that I was immature. In today's culture, we whine and complain and stomp our feet like little crybabies. Think about this for moment. Almost a billion people on the planet don't have access to clean drinking water. So many people live under communism and they don't have the freedom or the goods we have. Why are we so ungrateful?

Our culture is so immature. Let's not be that. If you want to become the person you were created to be, you can't live an irresponsible life.

Another occasion when I had to be mature enough to put Denise first was during a time when I was traveling constantly. Christian was young and Denise needed me at home but I had more "important" things to do.

I had my biggest business deal ever going at that time. There was a ton of potential profit and professional growth potential because of this deal. It was huge! I was about to leave for Salt Lake City the next day to consummate the deal.

I was talking to Denise on the phone the day before I was to leave, and the conversation turned really bad. I don't remember the actual conversation we had, but I remember how I felt when she basically said, "It's over."

I didn't even think about it for a second. I responded with, "The trip has been cancelled. I will be home." When I told Denise that, I hadn't even talked it over with my new business partner in Salt Lake, but I knew that my family was more important than any business deal.

Fortunately, my business associate was a family man himself and he understood. We did the meeting via conference call, and all was well. And that deal did change the course of my career. Committing to your family pays big dividends. Avoiding responsibility causes lots of pain and suffering. What outcome do you want? It's up to you.

Attractive – It's important to be attractive on the outside, but more importantly on the inside. When we get Hollywood out of our minds and we stop allowing the sex crazed media to shape our views of what relationships and marriage should be about, we begin to see the phenomenal value in another human being.

We are spirit beings that have a soul. We are housed in a corruptible body. No matter how good you or your partner looks today, it won't always be that way. If your attraction is merely physical, your relationship will be shallow and you won't experience the joy and fulfillment that comes from walking the journey of becoming who you were created to be.

The Word of God says, "Recognize no man according to the flesh." In other words, there are only two kinds of people; those that have God in their heart and those that don't. Saved or unsaved. When we see someone that knows God, that has the Holy Spirit inside them, we want to fan that flame. We want to encourage them to be all they can be in Christ.

When we see those that don't have Christ, we long for them to be reconciled to Him. The bible says we have "the ministry of reconciliation." It's hard not to look at other people's sin and define them by that. Don't get me wrong; when people are pushing sin on us publicly, we should fight for what is right. The Apostles did it, and so did our founding fathers. Don't dodge the responsibility to say what's right in order to not offend someone. Jesus offended many people. That's why they killed him.

At the same time, don't go out looking for trouble. Look for the gifts God has given others and help them to see their gift. If they know God, encourage them to live that life to the fullest. If they don't be that minister of reconciliation and help them reconcile to God.

The goal is to be attractive on the inside, not just the outside. But we should also be diligent to keep from letting ourselves go physically. We should do everything we can within out power to keep ourselves attractive for our spouse. The longer you are married, it seems that the more you're willing to be unattractive at home. Get up, dress up, and show up for your spouse.

Don't be a slob.

Responsible – Fulfilling our role in our marriage brings us closer to living out our purpose and potential. God says when we are faithful with a little; we can be faithful with a lot. We must be good stewards of what God has given us.

I've been a poor steward of finances in the past. Fortunately for me, Denise has always been good with money. I finally learned the hard way, and thankfully have become very successful financially myself, and I can now take care of Denise.

Remember that this entire book is about you *becoming* the person you were created to be. To find your purpose. To mold you. To shape you. That happens by committing to your spouse and loving your spouse.

When we are responsible with the relationships God puts in our path- with our finances, with the goods and services we are blessed with, as well as our bodies and our very souls- God will *bless* us!

Don't you want to be blessed? Of course you do! I can almost hear you saying, "But I have tremendous problems." My response: I know you do. Jesus had tremendous problems. He was so stressed out the night before He went to the cross, that he sweat *blood*. Did you hear that? He sweat blood. Have you ever sweat blood?

No matter what the enemy might bring us, no matter what the world might throw at us, no matter what you might bring upon yourself, love God, and love others. It always works. Love never fails and Phenomenal Love will take you over the top!

Respectful – Respect the gifts God has given your spouse. As we discovered in a previous chapter, we are different. When we come to value each other for who God has made them, our attitude changes. When I realize that God made my wife the way she is, it changes how I treat her. When we realize that even when people mess up, that they are special creatures made by God, we will treat them better. Do you really want to try and control, change, or mess with God's creation?

Inspirational – No one wants to be around someone who's negative. Being inspirational doesn't mean entertaining someone. It doesn't mean that you have to become a motivational speaker. What it means is to allow God to do the beautiful work in you that He wants to do. Discover your gift and purpose. Everyone has a gift. When you let your gift shine, it inspires others.

Godly love is inspirational. When you simply love someone in their love language, when they know you love them, they will be inspired. When you put them first, they will be inspired. People that love us and care about us inspire us all. Why? Because we know deep inside that God is working. It gives us hope that we can become the person we want to be also.

Even if your spouse doesn't respond, do it for yourself. Do it for God. Do it for those that will accept your gifts and be inspired because of it.

Available – Being there when your spouse needs you. Physically and emotionally. I have failed with this one, but I've gotten better. Recently, my wife told me I had "graduated" her program. In other words, I had become the man she wished to be married to. I thought to myself, "what do I do now?"

My wife has been superb at this one. She is *always* there for me, for our son Christian, and for everyone else! On the DISC Personality Profile, I have no S whatsoever. It's awful. But I manage to help a lot of people. I just do it differently.

Grateful – Zig Ziglar , who was joyfully married for 66 years, said, "Of all the attitudes one can acquire, by far the most important and most life changing is the attitude of gratitude." When you are grateful, you aren't focused on yourself.

Gratitude brings a great feeling with it. It brings a feeling of fulfillment. It creates joy. It brings the feeling that all is well. Selfishness doesn't exist when we are grateful. He also said "the more grateful you are for what you have, the more you will have to be grateful for."

Encouraging – Everyone wants to be encouraged. Encouragement means to have courage. To be discouraged is to be without courage. What kind of relationship do we have when we tear each other down? Build one another up and give one another the pure, the positive and the powerful fuel the other person needs to face each day with.

Mr. Ziglar said "Encouragement is the fuel that humans run on."

Conclusion

The Charge

Love is simple.

Love never fails.

God loves you.

Go and love.

Love God.

Love Others.

Love phenomenally.

Part 2
The Forces of Love
Brenda J. Sell

Forces of Love

Did you know that there is a supernatural Force of Love? It is inside of each one of us who are born-again, just waiting to be activated and released. It is documented in the Best-Selling Book of all time – the Bible . This Force of Love comes from God! In this teaching, you will learn how to recognize the qualities of love, the enemies of love, and how to release God's love in your relationships.

[1] Wikipedia/List of best-selling books

Chapter 1

What Is Love?

Love is not just a luxury, love is a need that is part of our spiritual DNA. I hold the Taekwondo title of the Highest-ranked female in the America's, actually outside of Korea, and the 2nd highest in the world. The key characteristic of a true martial artist is peace. Where does that come from? It may surprise you, but it comes from the ability to love.

Ancient warriors did not have firearms. They were expertly trained to battle with their bare hands and feet. These warriors were bred to protect their communities. They were the heroes who loved their country, leaders, family, and the people. LOVE was the motivating source to develop their warrior skills.

Ancient martial artist would study the habits of wildlife to learn how to fight. You see, people are NOT born with the fighting instinct like animals, we were born to LOVE.

The first step to true happiness is to discover LOVE. Let's begin with the definition and understand of What Love Is!"

Love – unselfish commitment. To give without expecting anything in return. A strong, tender, compassionate devotion to the well-being of someone else.

In this teaching, we will study about God's kind of love. His love is unconditional. It sees and believes the best in others. You will learn how to recognize the qualities of love, the enemies of love, and how to release God's love in your relationships.

Love is a powerful force. We were created with a NEED for love, everyone needs love.

To operate in love, you must learn how to give and receive. That statement may be a surprise to you but it's true. You can't give away something that you do not possess. So how do you find love? You start with the source.

God is love. It's not just that He possesses love, HE IS LOVE, that is who He is! He is the source. This is a critical fact to grasp if you want to experience true love. The first step to finding love is to develop a relationship with God who is the source. The Bible calls this to be "born-again[1]." (More on how at the end of this teaching.) When you were born again, God put Himself and His own nature of love inside of you. Romans 5 says: *"He poured out His love in your heart through the Holy Spirit."* Genuine love (love that comes from God) comes from a heart overflowing with affection for God, freeing us to seek another person's best interest, even over our own. As you develop a personal relationship with God, He teaches you to love His way. You begin to see people through His eyes, you begin to feel His heartbeat for others. You become a carrier of supernatural love. His love compels you to love others!

"For the love of Christ controls us.[2]"

One of the Greek words for love is agape: It means unselfish commitment. Indicates a choice to serve God, to love your neighbor, to accept yourself, without expecting something in return. It is unconditional.

Our study of love is on the agape love, sometimes referred to as the God-kind of love. John 3:16 describes the fullness of God's love.

"For God so loved the world that he gave his only Son, so that everyone who believes in Him will not perish, but have eternal life." Out of God's love for mankind, He GAVE His very best – His Son, our Lord and Savior, Jesus Christ. Christian love is based on the deliberate choice of the lover rather than the worthiness of the one loved[3].

[1] The Bible: John 3:1-21
[2] 2 Corinthians 5:14a
[3] 1 Corinthians 13:1-13

Many people think that love is just an emotion or good feeling. That is not true. It's just the opposite, our emotions respond TO love. Love is an unselfish commitment. The kind of love we are studying is a verb, not a noun. It is an action, not a state of being.

Memory Verse: *"I am giving you a new commandment, that you love one another; just as I have loved you, that you also love one another." John 13:34 NASB*

Time to Study: Love is a Powerful Force

Agape love, God's love, is a new kind of power. It makes you the master of every situation. As long as you walk in love, you cannot be hurt and you cannot fail. The Bible says: "No weapon that is formed against you will prosper."[4] No one even has the power to hurt your feelings, because you are not ruled by feelings but by God's love. You are loving as He loves through you. Galatians 2:20 teaches us that as Christians we are "crucified with Christ".

"I have been crucified with Christ; and it is no longer I who live, but Christ lives in me; and the life which I now live in the flesh I live by faith in the Son of God, who loved me and gave Himself up for me."

I did a word study on this scripture one time, and it changed my life. I discovered that if I am dead, if I am crucified with Christ, as a dead person I have no feelings of my own. I can't be hurt! I have a greater calling. I now live my life for Christ , by His strength. It is not really my life; it is His life. I gave it to Him. It is a life of faith in Christ, who loved me, and made it possible for me to live by faith. His love for me makes it possible to give Him everything I have. I can trust Him. He has proven His love for me. He gives me everything I need to overcome the hurts and pains that come in developing relationships. A friend of mine once said, *"it is better to have loved and been hurt, than to have never experienced love at all."* I can take a risk in loving other people because the love of God sustains me in all circumstances. Love is a powerful force. We must walk in love!

"For the whole Law is fulfilled in one word, in the statement: 'YOU

[4] Isaiah 54:17

SHALL LOVE YOUR NEIGHBOR AS YOURSELF.' But if you bite and devour one another, take care that you are not consumed by one another.[5]" All of life circles around relationships. The way you treat people WILL have an effect on you.

Love God and Love Others

Jesus was asked what the greatest commandment was. His answer is found in *Matthew 22: 37-39*

"...YOU SHALL LOVE THE LORD YOUR GOD WITH ALL YOUR HEART, AND WITH ALL YOUR SOUL, AND WITH ALL YOUR MIND. This is the great and foremost commandment. The second is like it, YOU SHALL LOVE YOUR NEIGHBOR AS YOURSELF."

All of the other commandments in the Bible are summed up in loving God with all your heart and loving others as yourself. I must make a decision that everything I have is His. He becomes my reason for living, my source of life. All that I have; my hopes, my dreams, my ambitions, I give to Him. With all my heart, I surrender to His will in my life. With all my soul, I focus my thoughts on His love for me. With all my mind I choose to walk in obedience to His Word. Love is a lifestyle of giving a lifestyle of worship to the Lord. Giving all that we have to the Lord. Out of giving Him all we have; He gives us the heart we need to love others with that same unconditional love He gives us. He empowers us to love others with His love that flows through us.

Love Is Committed

Love is developed through commitment. Love is not an emotion. Love is committed; it endures and looks after the best interest of others. Love is not selfish. Action causes reaction. You can't love in speech only, love requires action. When you run out of your love, hook up and allow God's love to empower your love.
Love cares – from the heart.
Love is unconditional.

[5] Galatians 5:14,15NIV

Love is obedient.

E.W. Kenyon says that agape love is a new kind of selfishness. You no longer seek your own success, yet your success is guaranteed! This love is revolutionary. If we fully understood the great return from living in God's love, we'd probably be competing with each other, each of us trying to love the other more. Can you imagine people competing to see who can love the other one more? Everyone would come out of the competition a winner. We'd be consistently sowing love everywhere. The Bible teaches us that life has a harvest - you reap what you sow. Our return, (the Law of the Sower[6],) would be so great, we couldn't even be able contain all of the blessings. God gives us love seeds to sow. When we sow love, we harvest love and we bless God as we love others.

The Fruit of the Spirit is Love

"But the fruit of the Spirit is ***love****, joy, peace, patience, kindness, goodness, faithfulness, gentleness, self-control: against such there is no law.*[7]"

The fruit of the Spirit is love. Love is the first fruit listed, but all of the others are only possible as we yield to love. Everything we do must be motivated by love.

Love includes all of the fruit.

Joy is love's strength.
Peace is love's security
Longsuffering (Patience) is love's patience.
Gentleness is love's conduct.
Goodness is love's character.
Faith is loves confidence.
Meekness is love's humility.
Temperance (Self-control) is love's victory.

Something to think about......

[6] Bible: Matthew 13:1-9
[7] Galatians 5: 22,23

Do you have relationships in your life that need repaired? Are you holding back on building new relationships because of hurts in the past? Are you willing to let God be your **source** of love? A person who refuses to love is missing out on the very best God has to offer. Don't YOU miss out on any of it. Release love every moment into every situation, every prayer and every thought, until it totally consumes your life. **GO FOR IT!**

The more you fellowship with God, the more you are changed by His presence and empowered to walk in love. The more you walk in love, the more intimate your fellowship with Him becomes. Love will strengthen you and cast out every fear that has robbed you of God's greater blessings. It'll drive the devil out of your affairs and set you free from every fear and torment of darkness.

Something to do........

The Word of God enables you to love people unconditionally. When you are a born-again Christian, love is already in you – you can't say you don't have love. It is a part of your new nature, your supernatural, natural disposition. You determine whether or not to love. Love flows out of you as an overflow when you spend time with God. Letting go of past hurts isn't easy. It requires you to have courage. It requires you to let go of those hurts and to trust. It begins when you trust God to heal your broken heart.

1 John 4:18 says *"There is no fear in love; but perfect love drives out fear: because fear involves punishment, and the one who fears is not perfected in love."*

Fear will paralyze the actions of love. Step out! Let the love of God cast fear out of your life. As you love Him and let His love fill your life, He will give you faith in His abilities to bring you through every circumstance of your life. Faith brings courage. Courage comes when you put your confidence in the Lord. He tells us he will never leave us or forsake us. That means He not only cares, but He always provides our every need. Be still before the Lord and sense the flow of His agape love, mercy, the wonderful love of Jesus coming up like a fountain from the Holy Spirit into your spirit. Then, love others with the love of God. If it seems too hard, remember, once you start releasing love into a situation, Jesus becomes responsible for its success.

Love never fails, and Jesus never fails! So, love your way to success.

Note: At the end of each section, you will find ***Speak the Word*** *declarations for you to say, out loud to declare and agree with what God says about you.*

Speak the Word...
I walk in love, and I never fail because love never fails!
"*Love never fails (never fade out or becomes obsolete or comes to an end).*[8]"

[8] 1 Corinthians 13:8

Chapter 2
Love Defined

"... God is love; and the one who remains in love remains in God, and God remains in him.

By this, love is perfected with us, so that we may have confidence in the day of judgment; because as He is, we also are in this world."
[1] **1 John 4: 16, 17** NASB

Let's explore the Bible definition of love.

First Corinthians 13 is sometimes referred to as the "love chapter." As Christians, everything we believe, every opinion we hold should always line up with the Word of God. The Bible is always the best standard to live by. 1 Corinthians 13:4-8 tells us precisely what the qualities of love are. This passage sets a very high standard for love; so high you might be tempted to think it's beyond your reach. But it's not! In fact, if you are a believer, that God kind of love (agape love) is a natural part of your supernatural disposition. It's in your heart now. You may not be yielding to it, but it's there.

1 Corinthians13:1-8
"If I speak with the tongues of mankind and of angels, but do not have love, I have become a noisy gong or a clanging cymbal. [2]If I have the gift of prophecy and know all mysteries and all knowledge, and if I have all faith so as to remove mountains, ***but do not have love, I am nothing.*** *[3]And if I give away all my possessions to charity, and if I surrender my body so that I may glory, but do not have love, it does me no good. [4]Love is patient, love is kind, it is not jealous; love does not brag, it is not arrogant. [5]It does not act disgracefully, it does not seek its own benefit; it is not provoked, does not keep an account of a wrong suffered, [6]it does not rejoice in unrighteousness, but rejoices with the truth;[7]it keeps every confidence,*

it believes all things, hopes all things, endures all things. [8]***Love never fails...***

Time to Study:
1 Corinthians 13 gives us a real good look at love. The world is hungry and looking for something that is real. They can spot a phony. If you claim to be a Christian, people will watch you and examine every move you make. You become a role model and mentor to others, even if you don't realize it. You are actually an ambassador, a representative of God's kingdom.

I remember sitting in church one Sunday morning and during the break after one of the worship songs I felt a tap on my shoulder a lady whispered into my ear and said, *"I want to thank you for saving my marriage."* I turned and looked and said, *"do I know you?"* She replied, *"No, I've watched you from a distance I sit quite a few rows behind you but, I've been watching you! I have noticed the way that you and your husband look at each other. I have watched the way that your son sits in the service, enjoying being with you and how he respects you. I determined that if God could do that for you, he could do it for me."*

You see, people are SEARCHING for God's love in action. They can they find that by watching you.

Love is Bold

Love is tangible; it is not just an emotional feeling; it is a spiritual thing that cannot be seen or touched. Love is evident to everyone who comes in contact with it, love gives and love leaves an impression with others, it points them to God.

My husband and I met a young man at a repair shop. As we began to talk with him about the Lord, we discovered he was a baby Christian. When he would talk about God, his face would light up, his body language changed, and he could hardly stand still. He told us that everyone at the shop teased him and called him "preacher boy." He said, "all I do is talk about Jesus and everyone thinks I know everything. They come to me with their problems and ask me all kinds of questions. I tell them what I know and when I don't know something, I just tell them I'm a new Christian and I'm still learning, but I know one thing - God has the answer." Praise God for people like this young man who is not ashamed of Jesus or the fact that he is a new but growing Christian. You see, the people he worked with noticed that something had changed in his life and they began to challenge that change. As they began to ask questions, he could have taken a cowards way out and been offended or denied his relationship with God. Instead, he responded in love. He was bold. He displayed his love for God by not denying Him. He displayed his love for his fellow workers by pointing them to Jesus!

Man Is A Spirit That Lives in a Body and Possesses A Soul.

The spirit is the real you, the part of you that lives forever. The spirit is the most powerful part of our being, yet it is the part of our being that is usually most neglected. When we are born again, the spirit of God takes up residence, or lives in our human spirit. The body houses our spirit and soul.

The soul is our mind, will, and emotions. **The soul is the major battleground.** We are in battle as we filter and fight what we allow our mind to feed on. The Spirit of God brings light through the Word so we can train our soul to come in agreement with God and walk on with Him and not be motivated by the things of the world, the flesh, or the devil.

Line up your thinking with what the Word says. Develop a dependence on God and renew your mind daily by studying your Bible and putting it into practice. What you feed grows, what you starve dies. Feed on the Word of God, and then act upon the Word. Be obedient to everything the Word of God tells you. If you love God, truly love Him, you will obey Him.

"The one who has My commandments and keeps them is the one who loves Me; and the one who loves Me will be loved by My Father, and I will love him and will reveal Myself to him.[1]"

We've got to get it into our will, (our soul) before we can act on it. Our soul makes the decisions on what we are going to do. We must have our heart enlightened and our understanding under the dominion of the man on the inside that is in contact with God, so we can agree with God. You must let

[1] *John 14:21*

your soul be in agreement with the Word before you can walk in the best He has for you. How do you do that? Be reading and meditating on God's Word. What you feed grows, what you starve dies. The way you think, is the way you become. Walking in love will then become a habit in your life.

The Nine Ingredients of Divine Love.

Listed below are the nine ingredients of divine love listed in 1 Corinthians 13 and practical ways to apply them.

Patient – It is not in a hurry, believes, hopes and endures all things. It always takes time to wait on God, to fellowship with Him. Let patience teach you to be patient with yourself and your weaknesses. Love is seen in us, as we are patient with each other. Look for opportunities to be a blessing to God and to others during trying times.

Begin by learning to be patient in little things. For example, how many times have you been in a hurry and had other people slow you down? Maybe you might be driving someplace and find yourself caught in traffic behind a v-e-r-y s-l-o-w driver. Take that opportunity to sow love through patience. Pray for that person! Just think, the devil meant for the traffic conditions to get you upset and you made a decision to use the delay to glorify the Lord by praying for someone else's needs and began exercising patience by using self-control to put the need of that s-l-o-w driver above yourself. Sometimes as I pass those slow drivers, I glance at them to see if they look nervous or upset to try to get a sense of how God may want to use me in my prayer life to bless them. Sometimes their hands are so tight on the steering wheel, I know that they are stressed and my prayers will help them make it through the traffic in safety and peace. Never underestimate the power of yielding to love.

Kindness –Never acts rashly, not inconsistent, puffed up or proud. Kindness looks for opportunities to bless others. Kindness sits and listens to the same story over and over again without complaining, condemning, or making the other person feel bad. Kindness stops the clock and looks a person in the face when they are talking to you instead of making them feel like they inconvenience you.

Generous – Giving, not envious or jealous. It always looks for an opportunity to give, ways to be a blessing to others as it serves God. There are many ways to give. You may say, "but I don't have anything to give." But that's just not true! Everybody has something to give. Give of your time, talents, money and possessions. A friend of ours is an immigrant from Cuba. He received his citizenship in the USA recently. His pastor knew of his attraction to Harley-Davidson motorcycles and bought him a Harley watch as a gift. Being from a communist country, he did not know about the love of God. This act of generosity, this act of love, showed this young man the love of God. Today he is serving God. The act of giving helped bring him into a relationship with the Lord. Every day, ask the Holy Spirit to show you how He would want to use you to be a blessing to someone else. Let love flow through you by being generous.

Humble – Works then retires, does not boast, and look for credit or attention. God uses humble men and women. Jesus continually humbled himself and we must follow His example. (Philippians 2:4,5) When we humble ourselves, He will exalt us. (1 Peter.5:6) Humility is quiet and content. When you are humble, you are satisfied that what you have done is pleasing to the Lord, nothing else matters.

My parents have been a great influence in my life, especially in teaching love by example. They have always been humble. They work hard, they watch over my family, take care of our home when we are on tour, watch over the office, and the list goes on and on and on. Yet with all they do, I have never one time heard them say to anyone how hard they work to help us. You see they have applied love through humility. They don't look for credit or attention. They take pleasure in helping us do the work of the Lord.

Courteous – Always polite, at home with all social classes, never rude, only looks for good in others. If we are to be used by God to reach the world, we must show respect and courtesy to others. Making fun of the way people dress, talk, live, or behave only builds a wedge. As Christians we are to build relationships, not cause separation. Look for the good in other people. You may not understand why they do things a certain way or why they live a certain way, but if you'll put those things aside and look for good, God will use you to be a blessing in their life. And when you're a blessing to others, you're a blessing to God.

Unselfish – Never selfish, sour or bitter, does not retaliate or seek revenge. We are so blessed to have people on our team who look out for our welfare above their own. My husband loves fried chicken. If we are going out to eat and the waiter tells us "we've only got one chicken dinner left" our team members are quick to cancel their order so that my husband can have his chicken. Being unselfish is a decision to bless others at the expense of not having what you want in order to be a blessing to someone else. It demonstrates love. Remember earlier when we said, "love is tangible?" Love is something that touches the heart of others. Give with a GREAT FULL (grateful) heart. Take pleasure in being a blessing to someone else. Rejoice with others when they are blessed. Fight off the thoughts of selfishness the devil will try to give you, by being SELFLESS, giving to others the things that you desire with a sincere appreciation for their success or blessing!

Good tempered – Never irritated. A person who loses control of their emotions automatically loses control of their actions. They do all sorts of things that do not honor God; cursing, ranting and raving, throwing things, sulking, fighting, talking down to others, complaining, talking contrary to what God's Word says about them and their life. You may be thinking there is no way I can be good tempered. I'm always losing my temper and I can't help it! You're right! There is NO WAY you can help it BY YOURSELF. You must enlist the help of the Holy Spirit. The Holy Spirit provides us with the power to overcome all of the attacks of the enemy. God is love. When we accept God's love in our life, by faith we can access whatever we need. Faith comes by hearing and hearing the Word of God. Look at that again. Faith comes by hearing ***and hearing*** the Word of God. That means more than once. We must renew or change the input into our mind. Then, our thoughts and disposition will change. Our character becomes more like Jesus. Start today! Make a commitment to spend at least 5 minutes a day in the Word of God and watch your life change.

Righteous – Hates sin, always gladdened by goodness toward others, never glad when others go wrong, always slow to expose, eager to believe the best, always hopeful, enduring. Righteous means right standing with God. Love is a heart that seeks after God and is willing to love others in spite of their wrong doings. There's an old saying: "Love the sinner, but hate the sin." Jesus lived this way. He was often criticized for hanging out with ex-prostitutes, adulterers, and all types of ungodly people. He often used the criticism to expose the evil intents of the accusers. Righteousness guards the words that are spoken. There is power in our words. When someone speaks to you in a negative way about someone else, ask yourself, "Why are they telling me this"? What good will come of it? What can I say or do that will prevent this from being gossip? How can I help? Let God use you to teach others how to be righteous by controlling what they say in your presence. The Bible says we are accountable for every idle word. That makes me nervous! If I am accountable for every idle word, how much more accountable am I going to be for deliberate words? Be careful what you say and be careful how you listen. Look for good and keep a right standing with God.

Sincere – Never boastful or conceited, not a hypocrite, always honest, leaves no impression except what is true, never self- assertive, does not blaze out in passionate anger, nor broods over wrongs, always just, joyful and truthful, knows how to be silent, full of trust, always present. Love is sincere.

When you love by God's love, you REALLY care about people. The other components of love form into sincerity. You know you have accomplished this when people TRUST you.

A friend called me one day in total panic, doing things that could be disastrous to her at that moment. She said to me, "I NEED to talk to you, BUT I NEVER want you to bring this back up to me again!" She was sincere and knew that I was also sincere in my commitment as a friend to be there when she needed me without condemnation. I listened and quietly prayed as she was talking asking the Holy Spirit to guide me. When we hung up, I prayed for her – not just a quick "by the way Lord" type of prayer, but a sincere prayer. You can do the same thing too! You can HEAR from God as you are sincere.

Something to think about......

Love gives at the expense of self; lust gets at the expense of others. This statement will help you in determining the motives of people. Think about it! Love gives - lust gets. Evaluate your own purposes. What are your motives? Are you looking to give? Or get? Without the constant influence of the Spirit of God and the Word of God, you will have a natural pull toward selfishness. Overcome that pull by meditating on the Word of God and then applying love in every situation.

We all have a natural mind that has been trained to believe things like, "You have to look out for yourself… and if you don't stick up for your own rights, no one will." On top of that, the devil continually works full time to draw us out of love, because he knows if he succeeds, he can pull the plug on your faith and steal the answers to your prayers. In short, you can make a "place " for the devil when you don't resist his thoughts and actions in your life. ©
GOD IS LOVE!

When you look at the definition of agape love and cross-reference it with *John 10:10* you see that God's goal is to bless you. He is your Heavenly Father. He cares for you, He IS LOVE. He is patient and kind. He endures long. His character IS the fruit of the Spirit. You realize that the purpose of Satan is to rob you of the love God has for you and is available to work IN you. Satan's mission is to steal, kill, and destroy. The good news is that God's love is stronger than the weapons of the devil.

God created man to have fellowship with Him. He provided the way through His son, Jesus Christ. When you accept Jesus as your Lord and Savior, you also reserve a place in heaven. You enter into a love relationship with God that causes you to be obedient to His will in your life. When you make Him the Lord or boss of your life, you are guaranteed eternal life. You become a child of God. You become a Kings Kid! You have an inheritance. That security gives you peace and confidence in God. You don't get to heaven by works, the work has already been done. Jesus paid the price!

You have authority over the devil and all evil that would try to destroy you. You have a purpose. You have a call on your life - to love God and to love others. Knowing all this, you are able to be sincere and true to your commitment to our Lord and Savior, Jesus Christ. God's love is endless, it is unconditional, and it is placed inside of you when you accept Jesus as your Lord and Savior.

Something to do.........

Set a goal. Set a goal to walk in love, to have your life ordered by and overflowing with the love of God. Love is noticed and experienced by others through you. Zig Ziglar says when we set goals you should always ask yourself "is my decision going to hurt anyone else?" Asking yourself this kind of question helps you determine if you are walking in love. Human love is so changeable, it can turn to hate overnight. It can behave affectionate one minute and then with rage the next and be called "love".

The bottom line is Love is the foundation for the Christian life. When you walk in love, you put yourself in a position where God Himself can protect you. When you quit seeking your own, He seeks your own for you. He is a great One to have on your side, because when He is for you, no one can stand against you.[2] Love is your one and only commandment. Love is the key to God's wisdom, power and protection. So, make it your personal goal to walk in love, to live in love, and to handle every situation in love.

Speak the Word...

I eagerly pursue and seek to acquire love.
I make it my aim and my great quest in life.

"Pursue love..." 1 Corinthians 14:1a

[11] Romans 8:31-34

Chapter 3

The Enemies of Love

"The thief comes only to steal and kill and destroy; I came so that they would have life, and have it abundantly." John 10:10

Time to Study: Enemies Of Love

Knowing that love is the most powerful force gives us a clue or insight as to why Satan fights so hard to steal it from us. A person who has not accepted Jesus as their Lord and Savior cannot fully love because the love of God is not in them. God is love. He is the source. Yes, an unsaved person can love, but not the same way a Christian can; because they don't have access to the source yet. This is one of the reasons we are told not to be unequally yoked in <u>any</u> relationship. Any relationship includes close friendships, dating, business partners, marriage partners and more. An unequally yoked relationship sets you up for conflict and discontentment. There are many enemies of love. They include discontentment, strife, envy, fear, worry, pride, jealousy, arrogance, rudeness, selfishness, being touchy, resentful, unforgiving, and bitterness.

Strife has many dangers. But one serious consequence to walking in strife is that it will hinder your prayers by robbing you of one of the greatest promises ever given to us. You can find that promise in *Matthew 18:19: "Again, I say unto you, that if two of you agree on earth about anything that they may ask, it shall be done for them by my Father who is in heaven."*

The devil hates agreement between believers. Agreement opens the windows of heaven to us, and it closes the door on every destructive thing he can do. So, he will continually try to disrupt that agreement by causing strife and division in the two places where believers come together in the most powerful way: - the family and the church.

You may not have thought of your family as a powerful force for God, but it is, if you're in agreement with one another. So, make it your goal to stay out of strife and walk in love at home. Many times, home is the most difficult place to be loving. At home, we tend to put our guard down. We're not worried about impressing anyone. Nothing will stop you from being selfish – except your commitment to walk in the love of God. Don't be fooled into thinking it doesn't matter how you act at home. It matters a great deal.

Make a commitment to keep strife out of your home. Learn to live a lifestyle of agreement with your spouse, your children, or your parents. See to it that your prayers prevail by being in harmony with your family members. The minute you mess up and get in strife, make it right. Say to the other person, *"Please forgive me. I love you. I don't want to be in strife with you."* Then say to the Lord, *"Father, I repent of that. I'm not going to be a person who is full of strife. I refuse to yield to strife. I choose to walk in love."*

You may have to repent quite a bit at first because you've probably developed habits that will take a while to change. But don't get disgusted and give up. Just keep acting on the Word, and you'll continue to mature in love.

Envy - a feeling of discontent and ill will because of another's advantages, possessions or success. The Bible talks repeatedly about the hazards of letting envy and strife in our life. Galatians 5 calls them the "works of the flesh." The works of the flesh are direct opposites to the works of the spirit. There is a battle taking place in the spiritual realm. The battleground begins in our thought life. Envy begins as a feeling of uneasiness, a mild case of jealousy. It seems harmless at first.

That's because Satan tries to sneak in the backdoor of our minds. He knows he probably could not get away with just putting the thought of hating someone else into action for no reason. He sets the stage for discord by creating uneasiness around others because of their position, possessions or success. Maybe someone has a new car, a baby, a place in ministry you would like to have, or a good paying job that you've been wanting for a long time.

Instead of being happy for them you begin to feel bad and get critical and upset. That opens the door for you to develop a critical spirit and begin to look for faults in their life. Your focus turns to what you don't have instead of what you do have. Eventually the seed of envy turns into strife, discord, and even hatred. The seed grew. The seed principle is that when you plant a seed, it multiplies. It all begins in your mind. God has given us tools to fight. 2 Corinthians 10:5 tells us to "cast down imaginations." In other words, take control of your thought life and to focus our thoughts on the good, not the bad. *Matthew 6:33* tells us to *"seek first His kingdom and His righteousness and ALL these things will be provided to you."*

Our minds are like sponges, they absorb whatever we feed them. What you feed grows, and what you starve dies. It's important that we guard our mind. Criminals will tell you that before they ever committed a crime, they thought about it, they saw themselves doing it, they talked about it, and when they finally did it, it was not a big deal. WHY? They had already committed the crime in their minds. Jesus said in Matthew 5:28 that the act of sin was not the first sin, they had already committed the sin in their heart. There is a process that takes place before our thoughts turn into actions. Motivational speakers give us this same formula for success.

1. Think it.
2. Meditate on it.
3. Say it.
4. See yourself doing it.
5. Do it!

Jealousy - suspicious, apprehensive of rivalry or resentfully envious. *Proverbs 6:34* says, *"Jealousy enrages a man."* Many marriages have fallen apart because of jealousy. Some people believe that if you love someone, you protect that love by being suspicious of everything other people say or do to the one you love. They think jealousy is a part of love. That is not true! Love trusts. It is not suspicious or resentfully envious. Jealousy is insecure and finds its identity in what it possesses. Jealousy must be in control. If a person is married to a person who is filled with jealousy, jealousy will always be suspicious of every relationship, conversation, and even the spouse participates in. A lady once told me that her husband was so jealous that if a car passed by and a man waved, he accused her of having an affair with the man. She lived a life of fear. She was always afraid to be nice, polite, or kind to others because her husband would accuse her of wrong doings and even punish her by physically abusing her because of the jealousy and insecurities that consumed him. Her advice was not to even date a man who is jealous. Jealousy is evil. It perverts' trust.

Pride - An overly high opinion of one's self, exaggerated self-esteem, or conceit. It shows itself through haughty or arrogant behavior. Pride is a difficult problem to deal with because it hides; it hides our thinking and causes us to deceive ourselves. Pride will not admit that it is present because it is too proud to do so.

Satan has no creative powers. He perverts what God has created and developed for our life. Pride is perverted humility. Pride keeps people trapped in a prison called self. There are only three people in this prison: "Me, Myself and I." It is really a lonely place.
Pride is all about I. Notice the I is in the middle of the word: pr**I**de? Interestingly, I is also the middle letter in sIn. Proverbs tell us Pride comes before a fall. It's evil and will not only hurt you, but it will hurt others too.

Pride hinders God from using people. It is mean to others, shows disrespect, is stingy and always demands to be first in everything. Pride wants to be seen, noticed, pampered, made comfortable, waited on, and put up front. The moment we start to think more of ourselves than we should, we need to humble ourselves before God and repent of pride. Choose to walk in humility instead of pride and your life will walking in love.

Bitterness, resentment, unforgiveness. These three things are devises of Satan and among the biggest obstacles to walking in love, especially among people who have truly been hurt or abused. Bitterness blocks God's blessing. *Mark 11:25* says © *"And whenever you stand praying, forgive, if you have anything against anyone, so that your Father who is in heaven will also forgive you for your offenses."* This is a commandment not a suggestion. It doesn't say forgive if you can. <u>It says forgive</u>! Let go of it! Forgive! If you don't, you are tying God's hands. Bitterness, resentment, and unforgiveness become a protective covering in your heart that will not allow love to penetrate.

You can never be happy, truly happy, until you break that evil force that has a grip on your heart. When you forgive, you turn that person over to God. "Vengeance is mine saith the Lord." Trust God to deal with that person. Refuse to let the wrong that others have done to you control your thought life. Your thought life is the doorway to your actions. What you feed your mind continues to grow, what you starve or refuse to think about dies.

Pray for your enemies and those who have hurt or abused you. Pray that God will convict them for their wrong doings and bring them to a place of repentance. Then, trust God.

When those feelings of resentment and bitterness begin to rise up in you say, "Satan, you're a liar. I have released the bitterness, resentment and unforgiveness from my heart. I trust God and I refuse to let my enemies rule my heart anymore! I have accepted God's love for me and I choose to walk in His love."

Forgiveness does not erase the past;
it brings closure.

Something to think about......

Examine your heart. Listen to your mouth, *"for out of the abundance of the heart the mouth speaks.*[1]*"* Your speech will help you locate what is in your heart. Are you walking in love, or in the enemies of love? Love is the real secret to success in relationships. It is important for us to study the Word of God to know what love is and what it is not. We need to study the enemies of love so that when the devil tempts us with them, we can quickly recognize his strategies and say, "No, devil! I refuse to do that. It's unloving, and I choose to walk in love!" Every step outside of love is a step in the flesh. We need to maintain a love attitude toward others. Make a quality decision today: I will walk in love!

Something to do.........

Many times, people harbor bitterness, resentment or unforgiveness towards

[1] Matthew 12:34

people for crimes they had no control over. A soldier came forward at one of our altar calls at a U.S. Army Base to forgive the murderer of his wife and daughter. The pain was so intense, he felt like he was dying himself. He knew he had to do something, so he joined the Army. He cried out to God for relief. God sent us. He responded. Running doesn't make it go away, only true forgiveness can.

Forgiveness does not erase the past; it brings closure. It gives you a new starting point. Some people refuse to forgive because they tend to think that if they forgive, it's like admitting there was nothing wrong with what happened, that it wasn't that big of a deal, or that they are accepting responsibility for someone else's sin. That's not true! That incident or series of incidents has robbed you of peace and love long enough. Satan wants you to believe these things so he can keep you in bondage, so he can continue to steal, kill, and destroy your life. You were a victim. Whether the criminal is living or dead, it's time to release the grip. If you let bitterness, resentment, and unforgiveness rule in your heart, they still have a grip on you.

God has provided freedom for you. Jesus said "I have come that you might have life, and life more abundantly." He is the healer. He is the giver of life. Let go - be set free. Now is the time for healing. Today! Don't let Satan rob you of one more minute of the abundant life. Forgive. Maybe you have cried out to God for relief, like the soldier did. God has heard your cry. He directed you to read this study so you can be set free. Say this prayer now:

"Father, I come to you in the name of Jesus. Your Word says that you are the healer of the broken hearted. My heart is broken. Your Word says if I will forgive those who have hurt me that you will hear my prayers and set me free from the terrible hurt that has held my heart hostage.

Satan, you're a liar. I release the hurt, bitterness, resentment and unforgiveness from my heart. Lord, I trust you and I refuse to let my enemies rule my heart anymore! I have accepted your love for me, and I choose to walk in your love.

Thank you, Lord, for setting me free. Help me to study your Word so that I may be strengthened and grow into the Christian, you want me to be. In Jesus name, Amen!"

Next, when the enemy comes in and tries to tell you that you really did not forgive, say "No, that is not true, I forgave, and I continue to forgive. It's in the past and I now live in the peace of God. I refuse to let my mind focus on the past anymore. Satan you're a liar. You have no hold on me. In Jesus name, Amen!" When Satan tries to remind you of your past, remind him of his future!

Congratulations, you've taken a big step of faith and courage. Now, take a deep breath and breathe in peace. Let the peace of God rule and reign in your heart. If you need to cry, cry, if you need to laugh, laugh. Take a few minutes to just rest in the presence of the Lord. Let God bless you!

Speak the Word....
I am not ignorant of Satan's devices. I determine to walk in love and refuse to allow him to take advantage of me.

"But one whom you forgive ANYTHING, I also forgive; for indeed what I have forgiven, if I have forgiven anything, I did so for your sakes in the presence of Christ, so that no advantage would be taken of us by Satan, for we are not ignorant of his schemes." 2 Corinthians 2:10-11

Chapter 4
Receiving Love

"But whoever follows His Word, in him the love of God has truly been perfected. By this we know that we are in Him: the one who says that he remains in Him ought, himself also, walk just as He walked." 1 John 2: 5,6

> *Did you know that there are literally millions and millions of dollars that people own but have never claimed? Sometimes they don't even know that they have it. Other times they refuse to receive it because someone left it to them, and they hold resentment, hatred, or bitterness against them. Still other times they don't want to do the conditions that would give them access to the inheritance.*

This is a true story about an elderly lady who was living in poverty. She had been a housekeeper to a very rich man. She couldn't read or write. But, she had a giving heart. She worked for this man and lovingly took care of him right to his dying day. When he realized he was dying he wrote her a note. That meant the world to her; so much that she framed it and hung it on her wall in the living room. Years later, a minister stopped by to visit the woman. As he looked at the framed note hanging on her wall, he asked if he could take it down and look closer. She said, "yes." He asked her if she would tell him about the note. She told the minister that she had taken care of this wonderful elderly man. Before he died, he gave her this note that was a precious treasure to her, so she framed it and placed it on her wall. Come to find out, the note was actually a very large check, he had left her an inheritance but she didn't even know it! The minister took her to the bank and sure enough, the check was good. The banker said he knew the old man had left his fortune to someone and was wondering when he or she would come in and claim it.

Like the elderly lady in this story, many people have an inheritance with God and don't even know it. Until you are born again you can't walk with God, your spirit is dead! But once you are born again you no longer have to live in spiritual poverty. We must learn how to receive.

Time to Study:

Defining Love

We've studied love and discovered that God is Love, and when you are born again, the love of God lives inside of you. We also discovered that according to 1 Corinthians 13 that the ingredients of love are in a package, not a list where we choose the ones that appeal to us. When we truly love, we are filled with ALL these qualities and strive to express them to all those around us. Love is patient, generous, not envious or jealous, is humble, courteous, unselfish, good tempered, righteous, and sincere. Love pays no attention to a suffered wrong. In Galatians 5:19-24 we learned that there are enemies of love and the Fruit of the Spirit are all issued out of love.

Applying Love

One day at the end of one of my classes a student came to me and asked me to pray for her. Her story broke my heart. She was in her 40's, married twice, three beautiful children, very outgoing and physically fit. She had just given her heart to the Lord a few months earlier. With tears rolling down her face she asked, "How do I receive love? I can honestly say that I have never experienced love before."

While ministering at West Point Military Academy, I was a guest in the home of one of the ministers. Alone in the kitchen, the minister's wife she asked me the same question. She knew how to give and help others, but had not learned how to receive and apply.

People are hurting and don't know how to stop the pain. Good News!!!!!! Help is on its way. Keep reading!

You Must Be Born Again.

The Spirit of God must dwell in you according to John 3:3 and Romans 10:9,10. **If you have not accepted Jesus Christ as your Lord and Savior, the Prayer of Salvation is at the end of this book. Turn there now to receive Him in your life and to be born again.**

Without being born again, you cannot receive the pure and perfect love that you've been longing for. **The God kind of love is inside of you when you are born again!** Only as we live in love can we fulfill the will of God in our lives. *2 Corinthians 5:17* says: *"Therefore, if anyone is in Christ, this person is a new creation; the old things passed away; behold, new things have come."* The foundation of this new nature is love. Love is the compelling force of our new nature. We always feel the need to love. Once you have received Jesus as your Lord and Savior, you are a child of God. His LOVE fulfills that need.

We Must Forgive Others.

Many who cannot or have not received love get stuck here. The God of the Bible, the God of the Universe is now your father, spiritually. He loves YOU! Yes, He loves you. He loves you in a pure, wholesome, righteous way! *Matthew 19:17* says, "*God is good.*"

"Every good thing given, and every perfect gift is from above, coming down from the Father of lights, with whom there is no variation or shifting shadow." James 1:17

Your Father God, has good and perfect gifts for you and He will not turn against you! If you have been hurt or abused by someone, there may be walls built up in your life to keep others out as a form of self-protection, like a shield. The shield protects certain parts of your heart so that nobody can ever hurt you there again. This is a natural thing to do.

The problem is, the shield blocks your heart from love coming in and from love going out. In order to receive love, you must be willing to be vulnerable to God. You must be willing to trust Him. You may say, *"but you don't know what I've been through, there is no way I can let go of the past and forgive that person!"*

I'm telling you that as long as you hang on to that line of thinking, that person from the past still has a hold on you! You must let go in order to be free. Forgiveness does not mean that what happened to you was okay, or that you accept what happened as good. No way! We have to start thinking like God. He is a God of mercy and of justice.

"The Lord says, "Vengeance is mine.[1]" "Now He said to His disciples, "It is inevitable that stumbling blocks come, but woe to one through whom they come! It is better for him if a millstone is hung around his neck and he is thrown into the sea, than that he may cause one of these little ones to sin.[2]"

When you hold bitterness and refuse to forgive, you tie God's hands from working in the situation and dealing with the parties involved.

"And whenever you stand praying, forgive, if you have anything against anyone, so that your Father who is in heaven will also forgive you for your offenses." Mark 11:25

You Do Have the Ability to Forgive

Refusing to forgive hinders or stops the flow of your prayers. Jesus made forgiveness a command, not a suggestion. Jesus didn't say, "When you stand praying, **try** to forgive" He simply said "Forgive." Period!

It would be unjust for Him to command us to do something we couldn't do. So, you can be sure it's within your power to obey His command and forgive – no matter how badly you've been hurt. Unforgiveness is dangerous. It will make your spirit weak and your prayers ineffective. It will pull the plug on your faith so much that you won't have enough power to move the molehills in your life, much less the mountains.

Don't allow bitterness to take root in your heart. Forgive, forget, release, let them go. We take responsibility for our life. You can't go through life blaming someone else for what happened in the past. Move on. Take

[1] Deuteronomy 32:35

[2] *Luke 17:1,2*

authority. Let the blood of Jesus cleanse you. Come against that depression, oppression, whatever has a grip on you and let the blood of Jesus cleanse you. In most cases, when you forgive and let go of them, the power of the devil is broken. There isn't anything that anyone has done to you, that you can't forgive.

Jesus Is Our Example

Jesus is our example. Even as He was tortured and hung on the cross, He looked down at those who had abused Him and refused to allow bitterness to rule him. He forgave them. Jesus came to earth as a man. He left all of His God privileges in heaven. Everything He did on this earth, He did in the power of the Holy Spirit, the same Holy Spirit that's available to you and me. In Hebrews it says He was thoroughly tempted in all points as you and I are.

That means He was tempted to have unforgiveness, bitterness, adultery, to lie, anything you have ever or will ever have to deal with, He overcame the temptation. He had a free will like you and I do. He could have chosen to yield to those temptations, but He didn't. He literally took our place as a man. He did not give in to any one of them. He demonstrated that you can live a victorious Christian life, walk in love, and be free from the power of darkness.

You Have A Choice.

That choice is to walk in love or to walk in unforgiveness. You can never experience complete love with unforgiveness in your heart. It's hurting YOU! God wants to set YOU free, but YOU must let him. Let go and trust Him! If you are ready to trust God and let go of your fears and hurts, say this simple but powerful prayer from your heart.

"Father God, I come to you in the name of Jesus. I trust you. I choose to receive your love in my life. By an act of my will I let go of the hurts and fears that have tormented me. I release them to you and I forgive the people involved, even though they don't deserve it. I determine to walk in love and to forgive others, even as God for Christ's sake has forgiven me. Thank you,

Lord, for setting me free and for giving me a clean heart. Amen!"

"Then Peter came up and said to Him, 'Lord, how many times shall my brother sin against me, and I still forgive him? Up to seven times?' Jesus said to him, 'I do not say to you, up to seven times, but up to seventy-seven times.'" [3]

The next time that thought of the thing you let go of comes up, refuse to feed it. Forgive again and move on.

Choose To Live the Higher Life.

God created man with a free will; He will never force us to do anything we don't want to. We choose[4]. We can choose to walk in the spirit realm or in the natural realm. Earlier we studied the contrasting works of the flesh and the fruit of the Spirit[5]. The lower life is the things of the flesh. A person who lives consistently in this lower life will not inherit the things of God.

"Now those who belong to Christ Jesus crucified the flesh with its passions and desires." Galatians 5:24

When a person gives their life to the Lord they are saved.

"that if you confess with your mouth Jesus as Lord, and ***believe*** *in your heart that God raised Him from the dead, you WILL be saved."* Romans 10:9

The word **believe** means; to cling to, to adhere to, trust in and rely on in truth. In other words, it means to make Jesus Christ the Lord or boss of your life. According to Webster's Dictionary, trust means to have a firm confidence in the honesty, integrity, reliability, and justice of another person or thing. When you put your trust in Jesus, you choose to have confidence is His honesty, integrity, reliability, and justice. You are saying you trust Him unconditionally and whole-heartedly with your life. You believe that everything He says is true. You choose to give up your hopes, dreams, and

[3] Matthew 18:21-22
[4] Deut. 30
:19,20
[5] As described in Galatians 5: 18 – 25

expectations and take His hopes, dreams, and expectations for your life in its place. You live an exchanged life. You give up your life, to live for him[6].

Your spirit and your flesh pull in conflict with each other. Romans chapter 8 talks about how the Spirit of Life makes us free from the tug of war. It cuts you loose from being dominated by the flesh. Make a choice to live in the higher realm. Resist temptation. Refuse to participate in the works of the flesh.

Do you want to give into the flesh or sell out to God and enjoy His level of life?

"Now those who belong to Christ Jesus crucified the flesh with its passions and desires. If we live by the Spirit, let's follow the Spirit as well." Galatians 5:24,25

Living in the spirit is a higher realm, walking with God. The fruit of the Spirit is evidence of our relationship with God. The Spirit of Life, Jesus Christ, is working in you. The inward man needs to be renewed every day through fellowship with God. As your spirit begins to dominate, your soul and body begin to obey God by practice. As a sinner you were good at it because you practiced it.

Get up in the higher realm of the spirit and you won't even desire the things of the flesh. When you are in the higher life, you have no desire for the lower life. Go after the things of God. Set your mind on spiritual things. When you're in the higher life, the lower life has no pull on you.

Something to think about......

The Tree of Ribbons

There was a man who was sent to prison as a teenager. When he had served his time to be released, he was well into his adult years. He knew that he had disgraced his family and did not want to hurt them anymore. When it came close to his date of release, he wrote a letter home to his family and told them that he would be riding the train that went by their house on a

[6] Luke 14:33

certain day and if there was a ribbon tied to the tree in the yard that would be a signal to him that it was okay to come home. If not, he understood that there was too much embarrassment and pain for his family and he would continue on without stopping. As he rode the train, an elderly man noticed his nervousness and said, "Son, I've noticed that you are very nervous and restless today. Is there anything you would like to talk about, or anything I can do to help you?"

The man said, "Yes sir there is. When we pass by my home, would you look and tell me if there is a ribbon tied to the tree? The ribbon is a sign of forgiveness for me and will tell me if I should get off the train or not." When they got near his home, the elderly man said, "Look, look! There is not a ribbon on the tree, it is a tree of ribbons, loaded with every color imaginable." The elderly man and his new found friend both cried. The man stepped off that train a free man. Forgiveness is an inseparable part of love. It breaks bondages of both parties.

"The one who does not love does not know God, because God is love." 1 John 4:8

Who do you know that needs to experience God's love? Pray and ask God how you could be used to bring His love to others. How about your family? What aspects of love can you sow to them?

Something to do.........

Love was deposited in you the day you gave your heart to the Lord. It's there! Now is the time to start tapping into it on a regular basis. Live a life founded on love. Walk in forgiveness, even if it starts off as a part of your everyday life. His mercies are new every morning. Take it one day at a time. Don't worry about what you are going to do or feel tomorrow. Concentrate on today. Start sowing love. Everywhere you go, look for ways to be a blessing to others in the name of the Lord. **LOVE is the foundation of VICTORY.** Love is patient, kind, endures, and never fails. When someone speaks a mean word to you, speak a word of love back to him or her. A soft answer turns away wrath. Without love, there is always failure. With love, you never fail, because love never fails! Look at your circumstances in the light of love. **Love is perfected in you as you**:

1. **Have living contact with God** (spending time studying the Bible, in prayer, in worship, growing in a church body, and in fellowship with other Christians.)

2. **Apply the Word.** The Word of God is food to your spirit and mind. There are two ditches that people fall into. A lack of knowledge (just not knowing), and hearing but not doing (not being obedient to what the Word of God says.) The Word of God gives you strength and builds your faith. It keeps you encouraged, motivated and focused.

Love works! Give it a place of importance in your life. Examine yourself to see if you are walking in love. You simply cannot walk in the spirit or be a spiritual person without being ruled by love. The quality of your life depends on it. Living a life ruled by the love of God is what opens us up to walk in the spirit and live in the highest measure of the blessing and power of God! Don't give up, love always wins! Galatians 6:9

Speak the Word…

I walk in love, and I obey God, because I love Him and have received His unconditional love.

"But whoever follows His Word, in him the love of God has truly been perfected. By this we know that we are in Him: the one who says that he remains in Him ought, himself also, walk just as He walked." 1 John 2: 5,6

Prayer of Salvation

The most important decision a person will ever make is who they will serve. Most people don't realize that **not** making a decision to serve Jesus automatically confirms their commitment to follow Satan. He is the god of this world.

In order to change our spiritual ownership, we must act according to Romans 10:9-11,13 which says: "that if you confess with your mouth Jesus as Lord, and believe in your heart that God raised Him from the dead, you will be saved; for with the heart a person believes, resulting in righteousness, and with the mouth he confesses, resulting in salvation. For the Scripture says, whoever believes in Him will not be put to shame. For EVERYONE who calls upon the name of the Lord WILL BE SAVED."

It takes courage to step out in faith and believe God. However, God has made available to us everything we need to survive and that includes the courage to make the commitment to serve Him. The Holy Spirit prepares our heart to receive the things of God. Jesus Christ provided the way by becoming the perfect sacrifice for our sins. God the Father accepts us into His family as we confess with our mouth and believe in our hearts that Jesus is our Lord.

If you haven't made the decision to serve Jesus, now is your opportunity. This is the most important step you'll ever take in your entire life. You are a spirit being. Your spirit will never be at peace until you have made a commitment to serve God. Many have tried to find peace without Him, but all have failed. True peace comes from God.

If you have not been born-again, the Holy Spirit is speaking to you. Right now, make the decision to receive Jesus as your Lord and Savior. Sincerely say the following prayer out loud. If your relationship with Jesus is secure, study the following prayer and be prepared to let God use you to bring others into the Kingdom of God.

Prayer of Salvation

Father God, I know that I'm a sinner, but I don't want to be. I want to be a Christian. I want to be born again. I want to start my life all over again. Please forgive my sins. Lord Jesus, come into my heart and take over my life and by an act of my will, I choose to make You Lord of my life, boss of my life. I put You in complete control. I'll do anything You want me to do. I'll be anything You want me to be. I'll go any place You want me to go. Your wish is my command. You are my Lord, the boss of my life. I believe in my heart that Jesus died for my sins and that God raised Him from the dead for my justification and I confess with my mouth that Jesus Christ is my Lord, the boss of my life. Father God, You said in Your Word that whosoever calls upon the Name of the Lord shall be saved and I'm calling on You now, so I know I'm saved. Thank you for saving me. I AM A CHRISTIAN.

Made in USA - Kendallville, IN
88290_9798404946680
02.08.2022 1438